Survival Communications
in the District of Columbia

John E. Parnell, KK4HWX

13 – ISBN 978-1478139300
10 – ISBN 1478139307

Cover design by:
Lynda Colón
FREELANCE GRAPHIC DESIGN &
MARKETING COMMUNICATIONS
www.hirelynda.webs.com

Titles available in this series:

Survival Communications in Alabama
Survival Communications in Alaska
Survival Communications in Arizona
Survival Communications in Arkansas
Survival Communications in California
Survival Communications in Colorado
Survival Communications in Connecticut
Survival Communications in Delaware
Survival Communications in Florida
Survival Communications in Georgia
Survival Communications in Hawaii
Survival Communications in Idaho
Survival Communications in Illinois
Survival Communications in Indiana
Survival Communications in Iowa
Survival Communications in Kansas
Survival Communications in Kentucky
Survival Communications in Louisiana
Survival Communications in Maine
Survival Communications in Maryland
Survival Communications in Massachusetts
Survival Communications in Michigan
Survival Communications in Minnesota
Survival Communications in Mississippi
Survival Communications in Missouri

Survival Communications in Montana
Survival Communications in Nebraska
Survival Communications in Nevada
Survival Communications in New Hampshire
Survival Communications in New Jersey
Survival Communications in New Mexico
Survival Communications in New York
Survival Communications in North Carolina
Survival Communications in North Dakota
Survival Communications in Ohio
Survival Communications in Oklahoma
Survival Communications in Oregon
Survival Communications in Pennsylvania
Survival Communications in Rhode Island
Survival Communications in South Carolina
Survival Communications in South Dakota
Survival Communications in Tennessee
Survival Communications in Texas
Survival Communications in Utah
Survival Communications in Vermont
Survival Communications in Virginia
Survival Communications in Washington
Survival Communications in West Virginia
Survival Communications in Wisconsin
Survival Communications in Wyoming

The above titles are available from your favorite online or brick-and-mortar bookstore or directly from the publisher at Tutor Turtle Press LLC, 1027 S. Pendleton St. – Suite B-10, Easley, SC 29642 or on our website: www.TutorTurtlePress.com.

TABLE OF CONTENTS

Appendix A – ARRL Affiliated Ham Radio Clubs in the District of Columbia

Appendix B – FCC Amateur Radio Licenses in the District of Columbia

Survival Communications in the District of Columbia

Perhaps you have prepared for WTSHTF or TEOTWAWKI with respect to food, water, self-defense and shelter. But what about communication?

Whenever there is a disaster (hurricane, earthquake, economic collapse, nuclear war, EMF, solar eruption, etc.), the normal means of communication that we're all reliant upon (cell phone, land line phone, the Internet, etc.) will probably be, at best, sporadic and at worst, non-existent.

As this author sees it, short of smoke signals and mirrors, there are three options for communication in "trying times": (1) GMRS or FRS radios; (2) CB radios; and (3) ham or amateur radio. Let's consider each of these options to come up with the most acceptable one.

GMRS (General Mobile Radio Service) / FRS (Family Radio Service)

GMRS (General Mobile Radio Service) / FRS (Family Radio Service) radios work optimally over short distances where there is minimal interference. Originally designed to be used as pagers, particularly inside a building or other such confined area, these radios are low-cost and convenient to carry. Unfortunately their small size and light weight comes with a trade-off – short range and short battery life. These radios are supposed to be able to communicate for up to 25-30 miles. Right. That's on level terrain, without buildings or trees getting in the way. While battery life technology is constantly improving, you will need spare batteries to keep communicating or someway of recharging the ones in the radio. In this author's opinion, GMRS/FRS radios are not first choice when concerned with medium or long range communication.

CB (Citizens Band)

CB (Citizens Band) radios operate in a frequency range originally reserved for ham or amateur radio operation. Because of the overwhelming number of people wishing quick, low-cost, regulation-free communication, the FCC (Federal Communication Commission) split off a portion of the frequency spectrum and allowed anyone to purchase a CB radio and start communicating. No test. No license. Just personal/business communication. Today, CB radios are readily available in such outlets as eBay and Craigslist. This author has seen them at yard/garage/tag sales and at flea markets.

CB radios come in a variety of "flavors." Fixed units, sometimes referred to as base units are intended for home use. For the most part, they derive their power from the utility company. In the event of loss of electricity, most base units can also be connected to a 12-volt battery, like that in your car/truck. If you choose to obtain a fixed unit, make sure you know how to connect the unit to the battery – ahead of time. Trying to figure this out when you're under extra stress is not a good situation.

A second type of CB radio is designed to be mobile, that is, installed in your car/truck. It gets its power from the vehicle's battery. You can either attach an antenna permanently to the vehicle or have a removable, magnetic type antenna.

The third type of CB radio is designed for handheld use. They are small and light. Most weigh less than a pound and operate on batteries. Yes, using batteries in a CB poses the same limitations as those by the GMRS/FRS radios, but have the added advantage that most handheld units come with a cigarette lighter adapter. Comes in handy when you are on the move and wish to be able to communicate both from a vehicle and also when you have to abandon it.

While they have a greater range than GMRS/FRS radios, CB radios are, legally, limited to operate on 40 channels, with a power rating of four (4) watts or less. Yes, it is possible to alter CB radios to get around these limitations, but not legally,

Ham/Amateur Radio

Ham/Amateur radio is very appealing. With a ham radio, you are not limited to less than 50 miles, but can communicate with anyone in the world (who also has access to a ham radio, of course).

Standardized Amateur Radio Prepper Communications Plan

In the event of a nationwide catastrophic disaster, the nationwide network of Amateur Radio licensed preppers will need a set of standardized meeting frequencies to share information and coordinate activities between various prepper groups. This Standardized Amateur Radio Communications Plan establishes a set of frequencies on the 80 meter, 40 meter, 20 meter, and 2 meter Amateur Radio bands for use during these types of catastrophic disasters.

Routine nets will not be held on all of these frequencies, but preppers are encouraged to use them when coordinating with other preppers on a routine basis. Routine nets may be conducted by The American Preparedness Radio Net (TAPRN) on these or other frequencies as they see fit. However, TAPRN will promote the use of these standardized frequencies by all Amateur Radio licensed preppers during times of catastrophic disaster. The promotion of this Standardized Amateur Radio Communications Plan is encouraged by all means within the prepper community, including via Amateur Radio, Twitter, Facebook, and various blogs.

Standardized Frequencies and Modes
80 Meters – 3.818 MHz LSB (TAPRN Net: Sundays at 9 PM ET) 40 Meters – 7.242 MHz LSB 40 Meters Morse Code / Digital – 7.073 MHz USB (TAPRN: Sundays at 7:30 PM ET on CONTESTIA 4/250) 20 Meters – 14.242 MHz USB 2 Meters – 146.420 MHz FM

Nets and Network Etiquette

In times of nationwide catastrophic disaster, the ability of any one prepper to initiate and sustain themselves as a net control may be limited by the availability of power and other resource shortages. However, all licensed preppers are encouraged to maintain a listening watch on these frequencies as often as possible during a catastrophic disaster. Preppers may routinely announce themselves in the following manner:

• This is [Your Callsign Phonetically] in [Your State], maintaining a listening watch on [Standard Frequency] for any preppers on frequency seeking information or looking to provide information. Please call [Your Callsign Phonetically]. Preppers exchanging information that may require follow up should agree upon a designated time to return to the frequency and provide further information. If other stations are utilizing the frequency at the designated time you return, maintain watch and proceed with your communications when those stations are finished. If your communications are urgent and the stations on frequency are not passing information of a critical nature, interrupt with the word "Break" and request use of the frequency.

For More Information

Catastrophe Network: http://www.catastrophenetwork.org or @CatastropheNet on Twitter The American Preparedness Radio Network: http://www.taprn.com or @TAPRN on Twitter

In order to use a ham radio, legally, one must be licensed to do so by the FCC (other countries have analogous governmental bodies to regulate ham radio). To obtain a license is quite easy – take a test and pay your license fee. There are currently three classes of license – Technician, General, and Amateur Extra. With each of these licenses come specific abilities.

Technician class is the beginning level. The exam consists of 35 multiple choice questions randomly drawn from a pool of 395 questions. The question pool is readily available online for free downloading (http://www.ncvec.org/downloads/Revised%20Element%202.Pdf) or in such publications at *Ham Radio License Manual Revised 2nd Edition* (ISBN 978-0-87259-097-7). The current Technician pool of questions is to be used from July 1, 2010 to June 30, 2014. Be sure the question pool you are studying from is current. You will need to score at least 26 correct to pass. (Do not worry, Morse Code is no longer on the test, although many ham operators use it anyway.) You do not need to take a formal class in order to qualify to take the exam. You can learn the material on your own. Most people spend 10-15 hours studying and then successfully take the exam. The cost of taking the exam is under $20. The exam is given in MANY locations throughout the US. Usually the exam is given by area ham clubs. You do not have to belong to the club to take the exam. Check Appendix A for a listing of clubs in The District of Columbia.

Topics for the Technician License in Amateur Radio

The Technician license exam covers such topics as basic regulations, operating practices, and electronic theory, with a focus on VHF and UHF applications. Below is the syllabus for the Technician Class.

Subelement T1 – FCC Rules, descriptions and definitions for the amateur radio service, operator and station license responsibilities

[6 Exam Questions – 6 Groups]

T1A – Amateur Radio services; purpose of the amateur service, amateur-satellite service, operator/primary station license grant, where FCC rules are codified, basis and purpose of FCC rules, meanings of basic terms used in FCC rules

T1B – Authorized frequencies; frequency allocations, ITU regions, emission type, restricted sub-bands, spectrum sharing, transmissions near band edges

T1C – Operator classes and station call signs; operator classes, sequential, special event, and vanity call sign systems, international communications, reciprocal operation, station license licensee, places where the amateur service is regulated by the FCC, name and address on ULS, license term, renewal, grace period

T1D – Authorized and prohibited transmissions

T1E – Control operator and control types; control operator required, eligibility, designation of control operator, privileges and duties, control point, local, automatic and remote control, location of control operator

T1F – Station identification and operation standards; special operations for repeaters and auxiliary stations, third party communications, club stations, station security, FCC inspection

Subelement T2 – Operating Procedures

[3 Exam Questions – 3 Groups]

T2A – Station operation; choosing an operating frequency, calling another station, test transmissions, use of minimum power, frequency use, band plans

T2B – VHF/UHF operating practices; SSB phone, FM repeater, simplex, frequency offsets, splits and shifts, CTCSS, DTMF, tone squelch, carrier squelch, phonetics

T2C – Public service; emergency and non-emergency operations, message traffic handling

Subelement T3 – Radio wave characteristics, radio and electromagnetic properties, propagation modes

[3 Exam Questions – 3 Groups]

T3A – Radio wave characteristics; how a radio signal travels; distinctions of HF, VHF and UHF; fading, multipath; wavelength vs. penetration; antenna orientation

T3B – Radio and electromagnetic wave properties; the electromagnetic spectrum, wavelength vs. frequency, velocity of electromagnetic waves

T3C – Propagation modes; line of sight, sporadic E, meteor, aurora scatter, tropospheric ducting, F layer skip, radio horizon

Subelement T4 - Amateur radio practices and station setup

[2 Exam Questions – 2 Groups]

T4A – Station setup; microphone, speaker, headphones, filters, power source, connecting a computer, RF grounding

T4B – Operating controls; tuning, use of filters, squelch, AGC, repeater offset, memory channels

Subelement T5 – Electrical principles, math for electronics, electronic principles, Ohm's Law

[4 Exam Questions – 4 Groups]

T5A – Electrical principles; current and voltage, conductors and insulators, alternating and direct current

T5B – Math for electronics; decibels, electronic units and the metric system

T5C – Electronic principles; capacitance, inductance, current flow in circuits, alternating current, definition of RF, power calculations

T5D – Ohm's Law

Subelement T6 – Electrical components, semiconductors, circuit diagrams, component functions

[4 Exam Groups – 4 Questions]

T6A – Electrical components; fixed and variable resistors, capacitors, and inductors; fuses, switches, batteries

T6B – Semiconductors; basic principles of diodes and transistors

T6C – Circuit diagrams; schematic symbols

T6D – Component functions

Subelement T7 – Station equipment, common transmitter and receiver problems, antenna measurements and troubleshooting, basic repair and testing

[4 Exam Questions – 4 Groups]

T7A – Station radios; receivers, transmitters, transceivers

T7B – Common transmitter and receiver problems; symptoms of overload and overdrive, distortion, interference, over and under modulation, RF feedback, off frequency signals; fading and noise; problems with digital communications interfaces

T7C – Antenna measurements and troubleshooting; measuring SWR, dummy loads, feedline failure modes

T7D – Basic repair and testing; soldering, use of a voltmeter, ammeter, and ohmmeter

Subelement T8 – Modulation modes, amateur satellite operation, operating activities, non-voice communications

[4 Exam Questions – 4 Groups]

T8A – Modulation modes; bandwidth of various signals

T8B – Amateur satellite operation; Doppler shift, basic orbits, operating protocols

T8C – Operating activities; radio direction finding, radio control, contests, special event stations, basic linking over Internet

T8D – Non-voice communications; image data, digital modes, CW, packet, PSK31

Subelement T9 – Antennas, feedlines

[2 Exam Groups – 2 Questions]

T9A – Antennas; vertical and horizontal, concept of gain, common portable and mobile antennas, relationships between antenna length and frequency

T9B – Feedlines; types, losses vs. frequency, SWR concepts, matching, weather protection, connectors

Subelement T0 – AC power circuits, antenna installation, RF hazards

[3 Exam Questions – 3 Groups]

T0A – AC power circuits; hazardous voltages, fuses and circuit breakers, grounding, lightning protection, battery safety, electrical code compliance

T0B – Antenna installation; tower safety, overhead power lines

T0C – RF hazards; radiation exposure, proximity to antennas, recognized safe power levels, exposure to others

Once your name and call sign are available in the FCC database, you have the privilege of operating on all VHF (2 m) and UHF (70 cm) frequencies above 30 megahertz (MHz) and HF frequencies 80, 40, and 15 meter, and on the 10 meter band using Morse code (CW), voice, and digital mode. For a Technician license in The District of Columbia, your call sign will consist of a two-letter prefix beginning with K or W, the number three (3), and a three-letter suffix. The single digit number in the call sign is determined according to which area of the US you obtain your first license. Even though you may move to another state, you keep this number in your call sign. This is also true should you upgrade to a higher license and get a new call sign. The numeral portion of your call sign stays the same.

Call Sign Numbers

Below is a chart showing the various numbers and the state(s) in which you would obtain the number.

Call Sign Number	State(s)
0	CO, IA, KS, MN, MO, NE, ND, SD
1	CT, ME, MA, NH, RI, VT
2	NJ, NY
3	DE, DC, MD, PA
4	AL, FL, GA, KY, NC, SC, TN, VA
5	AR, LA, MS, NM, OK, TX
6	CA
7	AZ, ID, MT, NV, OR, WA, UT, WY
8	MI, OH, WV
9	IL, IN, WI

Residents of Alaska may have any of the following call sign prefixes assigned to them: AL0-7, KL0-7, NL0-7, or WL0-7. Likewise, residents of Hawaii may have the prefix AH6-7, KH6-7, NH6-7, or WH6-7 assigned.

Once you obtain your Technician license, do not stop there. Go and get your General license.

General is the second of three ham license classes. Like the Technician license, to get a General license, you merely have to take a 35-question multiple choice exam and pay your license fee. Passing is still at least 26 correct answers and the fee is the same (less than $20). Again the question pool is available for free online (http://www.ncvec.org/page.php?id=358). It is also available in such print publications as *The ARRL General Class License Manual 7th Edition* (ISBN 978-0-87259-811-9). The current General pool of questions is to be used from July 1, 2011 to June 30, 2015. Be sure the question pool you are using is current. Being a bit more comprehensive than the Technician license, the General license usually requires 15-20 hours of study to learn the material. Check Appendix A for a listing of clubs in The District of Columbia where you might take your exam. Once your name and NEW call sign is listed in the FCC database, you're good to go. For a General license in The District of Columbia, your call sign will consist of a one-letter prefix beginning with K, N or W, the number three (3), and a three-letter suffix.

Topics for the General License in Amateur Radio

The General license exam covers regulations, operating practices and electronic theory. Below is the syllabus for the General Class.

Subelement G1 – Commission's Rules
(5 Exam Questions – 5 Groups) G1A – General Class control operator frequency privileges; primary and secondary allocations G1B – Antenna structure limitations; good engineering and good amateur practice, beacon operation; restricted operation; retransmitting radio signals G1C – Transmitter power regulations; data emission standards G1D – Volunteer Examiners and Volunteer Examiner Coordinators; temporary identification G1E – Control categories; repeater regulations; harmful interference; third party rules; ITU regions

Subelement G2 – Operating procedures
(5 Exam Questions – 5 Groups) G2A – Phone operating procedures; USB/LSB utilization conventions; procedural signals; breaking into a OSO in progress; VOX operation G2B – Operating courtesy; band plans, emergencies, including drills and emergency communications

G2C – CW operating procedures and procedural signals; Q signals and common abbreviations; full break in

G2D – Amateur Auxiliary; minimizing interference; HF operations

G2E – Digital operating; procedures, procedural signals and common abbreviations

Subelement G3 – Radio wave propagation

(3 Exam Questions – 3 Groups)

G3A – Sunspots and solar radiation; ionospheric disturbances; propagation forecasting and indices

G3B – Maximum Usable Frequency; Lowest Usable Frequency; propagation

G3C – Ionospheric layers; critical angle and frequency; HF scatter; Near Vertical Incidence Sky waves

Subelement G4 – Amateur radio practices

(5 Exam Questions – 5 Groups)

G4A – Station Operation and setup

G4B – Test and monitoring equipment; two-tone test

G4C – Interference with consumer electronics; grounding; DSP

G4D – Speech processors; S meters; sideband operation near band edges

G4E – HF mobile radio installations; emergency and battery powered operation

Subelement G5 – Electrical principles

(3 Exam Questions – 3 Groups)

G5A – Reactance; inductance; capacitance; impedance; impedance matching

G5B – The Decibel; current and voltage dividers; electrical power calculations; sine wave root-mean-square (RMS) values; PEP calculations

G5C – Resistors; capacitors and inductors in series and parallel; transformers

Subelement G6 – Circuit components

(3 Exam Questions – 3 Groups)

G6A – Resistors; capacitors; inductors

G6B – Rectifiers; solid state diodes and transistors; vacuum tubes; batteries

G6C – Analog and digital integrated circuits (ICs); microprocessors; memory; I/O devices; microwave ICs (MMICs); display devices

Subelement G7 – Practical circuits

(3 Exam Questions – 3 Groups)

G7A – Power supplies; schematic symbols

G7B – Digital circuits; amplifiers and oscillators

G7C – Receivers and transmitters; filters, oscillators

Subelement G8 – Signals and emissions

(2 Exam Questions – 2 Groups)

G8A – Carriers and modulation; AM; FM; single and double sideband; modulation envelope; overmodulation

G8B – Frequency mixing; multiplication; HF data communications; bandwidths of various modes; deviation

Subelement G9 – Antennas and feed lines

(4 Exam Questions – 4 Groups)

G9A – Antenna feed lines; characteristic impedance and attenuation; SWR calculation, measurement and effects; matching networks

G9B – Basic antennas

G9C – Directional antennas

G9D – Specialized antennas

Subelement G0 – Electrical and RF safety

(2 Exam Questions – 2 Groups)

G0A – RF safety principles, rules and guidelines; routine station elevation

G0B – Safety in the ham shack; electrical shock and treatment, safety grounding, fusing, interlocks, wiring, antenna and tower safety

With a General license, you can use all VHF and UHF frequencies and most of the HF frequencies. You would have access to the 160, 30, 17, 12, and 10 meter bands and access to major parts of the 80, 40, 20, and 15 meter bands. Of course, this is in addition to all bands available to Technician license holders.

Amateur Extra is the third of three ham license classes. Like the Technician and General classes, you merely have to pass a test and pay your fee to get your Amateur Extra license. This class of license is more comprehensive than the lower license classes. The exam is longer – 50 questions – and the minimum passing score is higher – 37. However, once you get your Amateur Extra license, all ham frequencies, VHF, UHF and HF are available for your enjoyment. The Extra exam covers regulations, specialized operating practices, advanced electronics theory, and radio equipment design.

Like for the other license classes, the question pool for the Amateur Extra license is available online for downloading (http://www.ncvec.org/downloads/REVISED%202012-2016%20Extra%20Class%20Pool.doc). It is also available in print form in such publications as *The ARRL Extra Class License Manual Revised 9th Edition* (ISBN 978-0-87259-887-4).

Topics for the Extra License in Amateur Radio

Below is the syllabus for the Amateur Extra Class for July 1, 2012 to June 30, 2016.

Subelement E1 – Commission's Rules

[6 Exam Questions – 6 Groups]

E1A – Operating Standards: frequency privileges; emission standards; automatic message forwarding; frequency sharing; stations aboard ships or aircraft

E1B – Station restrictions and special operations: restrictions on station location; general operating restrictions, spurious emissions, control operator reimbursement; antenna structure restrictions; RACES operations

E1C – Station control: definitions and restrictions pertaining to local, automatic and remote control operation; control operator responsibilities for remote and automatically controlled stations

E1D – Amateur Satellite service: definitions and purpose; license requirements for space stations; available frequencies and bands; telecommand and telemetry operations; restrictions, and special provisions; notification requirements

E1E – Volunteer examiner program: definitions, qualifications, preparation and administration of exams; accreditation; question pools; documentation requirements

E1F – Miscellaneous rules: external RF power amplifiers; national quiet zone; business communications; compensated communications; spread spectrum; auxiliary stations; reciprocal operating privileges; IARP and CEPT licenses; third party communications with foreign countries; special temporary authority

Subelement E2 – Operating procedures

[5 Exam Questions – 5 Groups]

E2A – Amateur radio in space: amateur satellites; orbital mechanics; frequencies and modes; satellite hardware; satellite operations

E2B – Television practices: fast scan television standards and techniques; slow scan television standards and techniques

E2C – Operating methods: contest and DX operating; spread-spectrum transmissions; selecting an operating frequency

E2D – Operating methods: VHF and UHF digital modes; APRS

E2E – Operating methods: operating HF digital modes; error correction

Subelement E3 – Radio wave propagation

[3 Exam Questions – 3 Groups]

E3A – Propagation and technique, Earth-Moon-Earth communications; meteor scatter

E3B – Propagation and technique, trans-equatorial; long path; gray-line; multi-path propagation

E3C – Propagation and technique, Aurora propagation; selective fading; radio-path horizon; take-off angle over flat or sloping terrain; effects of ground on propagation; less common propagation modes

Subelement E4 – Amateur practices

[5 Exam Questions – 5 Groups]

E4A – Test equipment: analog and digital instruments; spectrum and network analyzers, antenna analyzers; oscilloscopes; testing transistors; RF measurements

E4B – Measurement technique and limitations: instrument accuracy and performance limitations; probes; techniques to minimize errors; measurement of "Q"; instrument calibration

E4C – Receiver performance characteristics, phase noise, capture effect, noise floor, image rejection, MDS, signal-to-noise-ratio; selectivity

E4D – Receiver performance characteristics, blocking dynamic range, intermodulation and cross-modulation interference; 3rd order intercept; desensitization; preselection

E4E – Noise suppression: system noise; electrical appliance noise; line noise; locating noise sources; DSP noise reduction; noise blankers

Subelement E5 – Electrical principles

[4 Exam Questions – 4 Groups]

E5A – Resonance and Q: characteristics of resonant circuits: series and parallel resonance; Q; half-power bandwidth; phase relationships in reactive circuits

E5B – Time constants and phase relationships: RLC time constants: definition; time constants in RL and RC circuits; phase angle between voltage and current; phase angles of series and parallel circuits

E5C – Impedance plots and coordinate systems: plotting impedances in polar coordinates; rectangular coordinates

E5D – AC and RF energy in real circuits: skin effect; electrostatic and electromagnetic fields; reactive power; power factor; coordinate systems

Subelement E6 – Circuit components

[6 Exam Questions – 6 Groups]

E6A – Semiconductor materials and devices: semiconductor materials germanium, silicon, P-type, N-type; transistor types: NPN, PNP, junction, field-effect transistors: enhancement mode; depletion mode; MOS; CMOS; N-channel; P-channel

E6B – Semiconductor diodes

E6C – Integrated circuits: TTL digital integrated circuits; CMOS digital integrated circuits; gates

E6D – Optical devices and toroids: cathode-ray tube devices; charge-coupled devices (CCDs); liquid crystal displays (LCDs); toroids: permeability, core material, selecting, winding

E6E – Piezoelectric crystals and MMICs: quartz crystals; crystal oscillators and filters; monolithic amplifiers

E6F – Optical components and power systems: photoconductive principles and effects, photovoltaic systems, optical couplers, optical sensors, and optoisolators

Subelement E7 – Practical circuits

[8 Exam Questions – 8 Groups]

E7A – Digital circuits: digital circuit principles and logic circuits: classes of logic elements; positive and negative logic; frequency dividers; truth tables

E7B – Amplifiers: Class of operation; vacuum tube and solid-state circuits; distortion and intermodulation; spurious and parasitic suppression; microwave amplifiers

E7C – Filters and matching networks: filters and impedance matching networks: types of networks; types of filters; filter applications; filter characteristics; impedance matching; DSP filtering

E7D – Power supplies and voltage regulators

E7E – Modulation and demodulation: reactance, phase and balanced modulators; detectors; mixer stages; DSP modulation and demodulation; software defined radio systems

E7F – Frequency markers and counters: frequency divider circuits; frequency marker generators; frequency counters

E7G – Active filters and op-amps: active audio filters; characteristics; basic circuit design; operational amplifiers

E7H – Oscillators and signal sources: types of oscillators; synthesizers and phase-locked loops; direct digital synthesizers

Subelement E8 – Signals and emissions

[4 Exam Questions – 4 Groups]

E8A – AC waveforms: sine, square, sawtooth and irregular waveforms; AC measurements; average and PEP of RF signals; pulse and digital signal waveforms

E8B – Modulation and demodulation: modulation methods; modulation index and deviation ratio; pulse modulation; frequency and time division multiplexing

E8C – Digital signals: digital communications modes; CW; information rate vs. bandwidth; spread-spectrum communications; modulation methods

E8D – Waves, measurements, and RF grounding: peak-to-peak values, polarization; RF grounding

Subelement E9 – Antennas and transmission lines

[8 Exam Questions – 8 Groups]

E9A – Isotropic and gain antennas: definition; used as a standard for comparison; radiation pattern; basic antenna parameters: radiation resistance and reactance, gain, beamwidth, efficiency

E9B – Antenna patterns: E and H plane patterns; gain as a function of pattern; antenna design; Yagi antennas

E9C – Wire and phased vertical antennas: beverage antennas; terminated and resonant rhombic antennas; elevation above real ground; ground effects as related to polarization; take-off angles

E9D – Directional antennas: gain; satellite antennas; antenna beamwidth; losses; SWR bandwidth; antenna efficiency; shortened and mobile antennas; grounding

E9E – Matching: matching antennas to feed lines; power dividers

E9F – Transmission lines: characteristics of open and shorted feed lines: 1/8 wavelength; 1/4 wavelength; 1/2 wavelength; feed lines: coax versus open-wire; velocity factor; electrical length; transformation characteristics of line terminated in impedance not equal to characteristic impedance

E9G – The Smith chart

E9H – Effective radiated power; system gains and losses; radio direction finding antennas

[1 exam question – 1 group]
E0A – Safety: amateur radio safety practices; RF radiation hazards; hazardous materials

Once your new call sign is listed in the FCC database, you are good to go. For an Amateur Extra license in The District of Columbia, your call sign will consist of a prefix of K, N or W, the number three (3), and a two-letter suffix, or a two-letter prefix beginning with A, N, K or W, the number three (3), and a one-letter suffix, or a two-letter prefix beginning with A, the number three (3), and a two-letter suffix.

Ham radio equipment can be expensive or you can do it "on the cheap." The cost will run from a couple hundred dollars to well in the thousands, depending on what you have available. eBay, and Craigslist are good places to start looking. Most ham clubs do some sort of hamfest annually wherein club members or others are willing to part with older equipment. See Appendix A for a list of clubs in The District of Columbia.

Another excellent source of equipment, as well as advice on setting the equipment up and how to use it properly, is current ham operators. In Appendix B, the author has listed all the FCC licensed ham operators in The District of Columbia, listed by city, and then sorted by street and house number on the street. Who knows, maybe someone who lives close to you is a ham operator. Be a good neighbor, stop by and have a chat with him/her.

Like CB radios, ham radios come in three formats – base, mobile, and handheld. They can use the electric company for power, or operate off a car battery. In the opinion of this author, in spite of the slightly higher cost of the equipment and having to take a test to legally use the equipment, ham radio is the way to go when concerned about communication during times of crisis.

Canadian Call Sign Prefixes

Because of our proximity to Canada, many times ham contact is made with our northern neighbors. Below is a chart showing the origin of Canadian call sign prefixes.

Call Sign Prefix	Provence or Territory
CY0	Sable Island
CY9	St. Paul Island
VA1, VE1	New Brunswick, Nova Scotia
VA2, VE2	Quebec
VA3, VE3	Ontario
VA4, VE4	Manitoba
VA5, VE5	Saskatchewan
VA6, VE6	Alberta
VA7, VE7	British Columbia
VE8	North West Territories
VE9	New Brunswick
VO1	Newfoundland

VO2	Labrador
VY0	Nunavut
VY1	Yukon
VY2	Prince Edward Island

Common Radio Bands in the United States

Certain radio bands are more popular with ham radio enthusiasts than others. Below is a chart showing these bands and when they are most popular.

	Band (meter)	Frequency (MHz)	Use
HF	160	1.8 – 2.0	Night
	80	3.5 – 4.0	Night and Local Day
	40	7.0 – 7.3	Night and Local Day
	30	10.1 – 10.15	CW and Digital
	20	14.0 – 14.350	World Wide Day and Night
	17	18.068 – 18.168	World Wide Day and Night
	15	21.0 – 21.450	Primarily Daytime
	12	24.890 – 24.990	Primarily Daytime
	10	28.0 – 29.70	Daytime during Sunspot highs
VHF	6	50 – 54	Local to World Wide
	2	144 – 148	Local to Medium Distance
UHF	70 cm	430 – 440	Local

Common Amateur Radio Bands in Canada

160 Meter Band - Maximum bandwidth 6 kHz
1.800 - 1.820 MHz - CW
1.820 - 1.830 MHz - Digital Modes
1 830 - 1.840 MHz - DX Window
1.840 - 2.000 MHz - SSB and other wide band modes

80 Meter Band - Maximum bandwidth 6 kHz
3.500 - 3.580 MHz - CW
3.580 - 3.620 MHz - Digital Modes
3.620 - 3.635 MHz - Packet/Digital Secondary
3.635 - 3.725 MHz - CW
3.725 - 3.790 MHz - SSB and other side band modes*
3.790 - 3.800 MHz - SSB DX Window
3.800 - 4.000 MHz - SSB and other wide band modes

40 Meter Band - Maximum bandwidth 6 kHz
7.000 - 7.035 MHz - CW
7.035 - 7.050 MHz - Digital Modes
7.040 - 7.050 MHz - International packet

7.050 - 7.100 MHz - SSB
7.100 - 7.120 MHz - Packet within Region 2
7.120 - 7.150 MHz - CW
7.150 - 7.300 MHz - SSB and other wide band modes

30 Meter Band - Maximum bandwidth 1 kHz
10.100 - 10.130 MHz - CW only
10.130 - 10.140 MHz - Digital Modes
10.140 - 10.150 MHz - Packet

20 Meter Band - Maximum bandwidth 6 kHz
14.000 - 14.070 MHz - CW only
14.070 - 14.095 MHz - Digital Mode
14.095 - 14.099 MHz - Packet
14.100 MHz - Beacons
14.101 - 14.112 MHz - CW, SSB, packet shared
14.112 - 14.350 MHz - SSB
14.225 - 14.235 MHz - SSTV

17 Meter Band - Maximum bandwidth 6 kHz
18.068 - 18.100 MHz - CW
18.100 - 18.105 MHz - Digital Modes
18.105 - 18.110 MHz - Packet
18.110 - 18.168 MHz - SSB and other wide band modes

15 Meter Band - maximum bandwidth 6 kHz
21.000 - 21.070 MHz - CW
21.070 - 21.090 MHz - Digital Modes
21.090 - 21.125 MHz - Packet
21.100 - 21.150 MHz - CW and SSB
21.150 - 21.335 MHz - SSB and other wide band modes
21.335 - 21.345 MHz - SSTV
21.345 - 21.450 MHz - SSB and other wide band modes

12 Meter Band - Maximum bandwidth 6 kHz
24.890 - 24.930 MHz - CW
24.920 - 24.925 MHz - Digital Modes
24.925 - 24.930 MHz - Packet
24.930 - 24.990 MHz - SSB and other wide band modes

10 Meter Band - Maximum band width 20 kHz
28.000 - 28.200 MHz - CW
28.070 - 28.120 MHz - Digital Modes
28.120 - 28.190 MHz - Packet

28.190 - 28.200 MHz - Beacons
28.200 - 29.300 MHz - SSB and other wide band modes
29.300 - 29.510 MHz - Satellite
29.510 - 29.700 MHz - SSB, FM and repeaters

160 Meters (1.8-2.0 MHz)

1.800 - 2.000 CW
1.800 - 1.810 Digital Modes
1.810 CW QRP
1.843-2.000 SSB, SSTV and other wideband modes
1.910 SSB QRP
1.995 - 2.000 Experimental
1.999 - 2.000 Beacons

80 Meters (3.5-4.0 MHz)

3.590 RTTY/Data DX
3.570-3.600 RTTY/Data
3.790-3.800 DX window
3.845 SSTV
3.885 AM calling frequency

40 Meters (7.0-7.3 MHz)

7.040 RTTY/Data DX
7.080-7.125 RTTY/Data
7.171 SSTV
7.290 AM calling frequency

30 Meters (10.1-10.15 MHz)

10.130-10.140 RTTY
10.140-10.150 Packet

20 Meters (14.0-14.35 MHz)

14.070-14.095 RTTY
14.095-14.0995 Packet
14.100 NCDXF Beacons
14.1005-14.112 Packet
14.230 SSTV
14.286 AM calling frequency

17 Meters (18.068-18.168 MHz)

18.100-18.105 RTTY
18.105-18.110 Packet

15 Meters (21.0-21.45 MHz)

21.070-21.110 RTTY/Data

21.340 SSTV

12 Meters (24.89-24.99 MHz)

24.920-24.925 RTTY
24.925-24.930 Packet

10 Meters (28-29.7 MHz)

28.000-28.070 CW
28.070-28.150 RTTY
28.150-28.190 CW
28.200-28.300 Beacons
28.300-29.300 Phone
28.680 SSTV
29.000-29.200 AM
29.300-29.510 Satellite Downlinks
29.520-29.590 Repeater Inputs
29.600 FM Simplex
29.610-29.700 Repeater Outputs

6 Meters (50-54 MHz)

50.0-50.1 CW, beacons
50.060-50.080 beacon subband
50.1-50.3 SSB, CW
50.10-50.125 DX window
50.125 SSB calling
50.3-50.6 All modes
50.6-50.8 Nonvoice communications
50.62 Digital (packet) calling
50.8-51.0 Radio remote control (20-kHz channels)
51.0-51.1 Pacific DX window
51.12-51.48 Repeater inputs (19 channels)
51.12-51.18 Digital repeater inputs
51.5-51.6 Simplex (seven channels)
51.62-51.98 Repeater outputs (19 channels)
51.62-51.68 Digital repeater outputs
52.0-52.48 Repeater inputs (except as noted; 23 channels)
52.02, 52.04 FM simplex
52.2 TEST PAIR (input)
52.5-52.98 Repeater output (except as noted; 23 channels)
52.525 Primary FM simplex
52.54 Secondary FM simplex
52.7 TEST PAIR (output)
53.0-53.48 Repeater inputs (except as noted; 19 channels)
53.0 Remote base FM simplex
53.02 Simplex
53.1, 53.2, 53.3, 53.4 Radio remote control

53.5-53.98 Repeater outputs (except as noted; 19 channels)
53.5, 53.6, 53.7, 53.8 Radio remote control
53.52, 53.9 Simplex

2 Meters (144-148 MHz)

144.00-144.05 EME (CW)
144.05-144.10 General CW and weak signals
144.10-144.20 EME and weak-signal SSB
144.200 National calling frequency
144.200-144.275 General SSB operation
144.275-144.300 Propagation beacons
144.30-144.50 New OSCAR subband
144.50-144.60 Linear translator inputs
144.60-144.90 FM repeater inputs
144.90-145.10 Weak signal and FM simplex (145.01,03,05,07,09 are widely used for packet)
145.10-145.20 Linear translator outputs
145.20-145.50 FM repeater outputs
145.50-145.80 Miscellaneous and experimental modes
145.80-146.00 OSCAR subband
146.01-146.37 Repeater inputs
146.40-146.58 Simplex
146.52 National Simplex Calling Frequency
146.61-146.97 Repeater outputs
147.00-147.39 Repeater outputs
147.42-147.57 Simplex
147.60-147.99 Repeater inputs

1.25 Meters (222-225 MHz)

222.0-222.150 Weak-signal modes
222.0-222.025 EME
222.05-222.06 Propagation beacons
222.1 SSB & CW calling frequency
222.10-222.15 Weak-signal CW & SSB
222.15-222.25 Local coordinator's option; weak signal, ACSB, repeater inputs, control
222.25-223.38 FM repeater inputs only
223.40-223.52 FM simplex
223.52-223.64 Digital, packet
223.64-223.70 Links, control
223.71-223.85 Local coordinator's option; FM simplex, packet, repeater outputs
223.85-224.98 Repeater outputs only

70 Centimeters (420-450 MHz)

420.00-426.00 ATV repeater or simplex with 421.25 MHz video carrier control links and experimental
426.00-432.00 ATV simplex with 427.250-MHz video carrier frequency

432.00-432.07 EME (Earth-Moon-Earth)
432.07-432.10 Weak-signal CW
432.10 70-cm calling frequency
432.10-432.30 Mixed-mode and weak-signal work
432.30-432.40 Propagation beacons
432.40-433.00 Mixed-mode and weak-signal work
433.00-435.00 Auxiliary/repeater links
435.00-438.00 Satellite only (internationally)
438.00-444.00 ATV repeater input with 439.250-MHz video carrier frequency and repeater links
442.00-445.00 Repeater inputs and outputs (local option)
445.00-447.00 Shared by auxiliary and control links, repeaters and simplex (local option)
446.00 National simplex frequency
447.00-450.00 Repeater inputs and outputs (local option)

33 Centimeters (902-928 MHz)

902.0-903.0 Narrow-bandwidth, weak-signal communications
902.0-902.8 SSTV, FAX, ACSSB, experimental
902.1 Weak-signal calling frequency
902.8-903.0 Reserved for EME, CW expansion
903.1 Alternate calling frequency
903.0-906.0 Digital communications
906-909 FM repeater inputs
909-915 ATV
915-918 Digital communications
918-921 FM repeater outputs
921-927 ATV
927-928 FM simplex and links

23 Centimeters (1240-1300 MHz)

1240-1246 ATV #1
1246-1248 Narrow-bandwidth FM point-to-point links and digital, duplex with 1258-1260.
1248-1258 Digital Communications
1252-1258 ATV #2
1258-1260 Narrow-bandwidth FM point-to-point links digital, duplexed with 1246-1252
1260-1270 Satellite uplinks, reference WARC '79
1260-1270 Wide-bandwidth experimental, simplex ATV
1270-1276 Repeater inputs, FM and linear, paired with 1282-1288, 239 pairs every 25 kHz, e.g. 1270.025, .050, etc.
1271-1283 Non-coordinated test pair
1276-1282 ATV #3
1282-1288 Repeater outputs, paired with 1270-1276
1288-1294 Wide-bandwidth experimental, simplex ATV
1294-1295 Narrow-bandwidth FM simplex services, 25-kHz channels
1294.5 National FM simplex calling frequency

1295-1297 Narrow bandwidth weak-signal communications (no FM)
1295.0-1295.8 SSTV, FAX, ACSSB, experimental
1295.8-1296.0 Reserved for EME, CW expansion
1296.00-1296.05 EME-exclusive
1296.07-1296.08 CW beacons
1296.1 CW, SSB calling frequency
1296.4-1296.6 Crossband linear translator input
1296.6-1296.8 Crossband linear translator output
1296.8-1297.0 Experimental beacons (exclusive)
1297-1300 Digital Communications

2300-2310 and 2390-2450 MHz

2300.0-2303.0 High-rate data
2303.0-2303.5 Packet
2303.5-2303.8 TTY packet
2303.9-2303.9 Packet, TTY, CW, EME
2303.9-2304.1 CW, EME
2304.1 Calling frequency
2304.1-2304.2 CW, EME, SSB
2304.2-2304.3 SSB, SSTV, FAX, Packet AM, Amtor
2304.30-2304.32 Propagation beacon network
2304.32-2304.40 General propagation beacons
2304.4-2304.5 SSB, SSTV, ACSSB, FAX, Packet AM, Amtor experimental
2304.5-2304.7 Crossband linear translator input
2304.7-2304.9 Crossband linear translator output
2304.9-2305.0 Experimental beacons
2305.0-2305.2 FM simplex (25 kHz spacing)
2305.20 FM simplex calling frequency
2305.2-2306.0 FM simplex (25 kHz spacing)
2306.0-2309.0 FM Repeaters (25 kHz) input
2309.0-2310.0 Control and auxiliary links
2390.0-2396.0 Fast-scan TV
2396.0-2399.0 High-rate data
2399.0-2399.5 Packet
2399.5-2400.0 Control and auxiliary links
2400.0-2403.0 Satellite
2403.0-2408.0 Satellite high-rate data
2408.0-2410.0 Satellite
2410.0-2413.0 FM repeaters (25 kHz) output
2413.0-2418.0 High-rate data
2418.0-2430.0 Fast-scan TV
2430.0-2433.0 Satellite
2433.0-2438.0 Satellite high-rate data
2438.0-2450.0 WB FM, FSTV, FMTV, SS experimental

3300-3500 MHz
3456.3-3456.4 Propagation beacons

5650-5925 MHz
5760.3-5760.4 Propagation beacons

10.00-10.50 GHz
10.368 Narrow band calling frequency 10.3683-10.3684 Propagation beacons
10.3640 Calling frequency

Now that you have your license (you do, don't you?), and your equipment, you are ready to go live. Below is a suggested start.

1) Assuming you have the HT set up to the appropriate frequency, and offset, press the mic button on the HT and say, "KK4HWX listening." Replace the KK4HWX with your own call sign, the one assigned to you by the FCC (it's the law). If no one responds to your call, you may wish to try again. Hopefully someone will respond to your call.

2) Once you get a response, it will be in the form of something like, "KK4HWX this is ??1??? in Eastport returning. My name is Florence. Back to you. ??1???" then a tone. Let us examine the response more closely. She first acknowledged your call sign (KK4HWX), then identified hers (??1???). From the 1 in her call sign, you know that she first got her license in Region 1, meaning she got it while a resident of CT, ME, MA, NH, RI, or VT. She then told you where she's transmitting from (Eastport). The term "returning" means that she is returning your call. Her name is Florence. The phrase, "Back to you" indicates that she is turning over the conversation to you. She then repeats her call sign. The tone indicates to you that it is okay to proceed with your response. BTW if she had used the term "Over" instead of "Back to you," it would mean the same thing, just fewer words.

3) At this point, press the mic button and continue with the conversation. You should restate your call sign often during the conversation (perhaps every 10 minutes or less and whenever you begin transmitting). Don't forget to say, "Over" or "Back to you" whenever you are giving Florence control of the conversation again.

4) When you are ready to stop the conversation, you should say goodbye or use the phrase "73", meaning "best wishes." Your conversation would end something like, "??1??? 73, this is KK4HWX clear and monitoring." The "clear and monitoring" indicates that you are going to continue to monitor the frequency. If you are not going to continue monitoring, you may wish to end the conversation with Florence with, "clear and QRT" instead. The QRT means that you are stopping transmissions.

Call Sign Phonics

Because of different accents of various people, sometimes it is difficult to understand call sign letters when spoken. For this reason, most ham operators verbalize their call sign using phonics. Below is a table listing the accepted phonics for letters and numbers.

A = ALFA

B = BRAVO

C = CHARLIE

D = DELTA

E = ECHO

F = FOXTROT

G = GOLF

H = HOTEL

I = INDIA

J = JULIETT

K = KILO

L = LIMA

M = MIKE

N = NOVEMBER

O = OSCAR

P = PAPA (PA-PA')

Q = QUEBEC (KAY-BEK')

R = ROMEO

S = SIERRA

T = TANGO

U = UNIFORM

V = VICTOR

W = WHISKEY

X = X-RAY

Y = YANKEE

Z = ZULU (ZED)

1 = ONE

2 = TWO

3 = THREE (TREE)

4 = FOUR

5 = FIVE (FIFE)

6 = SEVEN

7 = SEVEN

8 = EIGHT

9 = NINE (NINER)

0 = ZERO

The words in parentheses are the pronunciation or the alternate pronunciations for the words or numbers, but you will hear both used. With the letter Z, (ZED) is by far the most commonly used. With the number 9, NINER is the most common and easiest to understand ON THE AIR.

If you wish to use Morse code (CW) instead of voice communication, the "conversation" would follow the same steps, with a few modifications. To type out each word would require a lot of typing and translating. If you are like this author, more means more, i.e., more typing means more typos are likely. To help with this situation, CW enthusiasts have developed a language all their own – they use abbreviations for common phrases. Below is a chart showing some of these abbreviations.

Abbreviation	Use
AR	Over
de	From or "this is"
ES	And
GM	Good Morning
K	Go
KN	Go only
NM	Name
QTH	Location
RPT	Report

R	Roger
SK	Clear
tnx	Thanks
UR	Your, you are
73	Best Wishes

Morse Code and Amateur Radio

If you wish to use CW, but are concerned about accuracy, you might consider purchasing a Morse code translator. This is an electronic device that you place in front of your speakers. It takes the CW sounds and translates them into English and displays the transmission on an LCD display. For the reverse, you can pick up a CW keyboard. With the keyboard, you type in your message and it converts the text to Morse code. The translator does not need to be attached to your ham equipment, whereas the keyboard would.

For your convenience, below is a table showing the Morse code signals and their meaning.

Character	Code
A	· —
B	— · · ·
C	— · — ·
D	— · ·
E	·
F	· · — ·
G	— — ·
H	· · · ·
I	· ·
J	· — — —
K	— · —
L	· — · ·
M	— —
N	— ·
O	— — —
P	· — — ·
Q	— — · —
R	· — ·
S	· · ·
T	—
U	· · —
V	· · · —
W	· — —
X	— · · —
Y	— · — —
Z	— — · ·

0	— — — — —
1	• — — — —
2	• • — — —
3	• • • — —
4	• • • • —
5	• • • • •
6	— • • • •
7	— — • • •
8	— — — • •
9	— — — — •
Ampersand [&], Wait	• — • • •
Apostrophe [']	• — — — — •
At sign [@]	• — — • — •
Colon [:]	— — — • • •
Comma [,]	— — • • — —
Dollar sign [$]	• • • — • • —
Double dash [=]	— • • • —
Exclamation mark [!]	— • — • — —
Hyphen, Minus [-]	— • • • • —
Parenthesis closed [)]	— • — — • —
Parenthesis open [(]	— • — — •
Period [.]	• — • — • —
Plus [+]	• — • — •
Question mark [?]	• • — — • •
Quotation mark ["]	• — • • — •
Semicolon [;]	— • — • — •
Slash [/], Fraction bar	— • • — •
Underscore [_]	• • — — • —

An advantage of using Morse Code is that when broadcasting CW, you are using reduced power, thereby saving your battery. Your battery is used only while actually transmitting or receiving.

International Call Sign Prefixes

As was stated earlier, all ham radio call signs begin with letters (or numbers) taken from blocks assigned to each country of the world by the *ITU - International Telecommunications Union,* a body controlled by the United Nations. The following chart indicates which call sign series are allocated to which countries.

Call Sign Series	Allocated to
AAA-ALZ	**United States of America**
AMA-AOZ	Spain
APA-ASZ	Pakistan (Islamic Republic of)
ATA-AWZ	India (Republic of)

AXA-AXZ	Australia
AYA-AZZ	Argentine Republic
A2A-A2Z	Botswana (Republic of)
A3A-A3Z	Tonga (Kingdom of)
A4A-A4Z	Oman (Sultanate of)
A5A-A5Z	Bhutan (Kingdom of)
A6A-A6Z	United Arab Emirates
A7A-A7Z	Qatar (State of)
A8A-A8Z	Liberia (Republic of)
A9A-A9Z	Bahrain (State of)
BAA-BZZ	China (People's Republic of)
CAA-CEZ	Chile
CFA-CKZ	Canada
CLA-CMZ	Cuba
CNA-CNZ	Morocco (Kingdom of)
COA-COZ	Cuba
CPA-CPZ	Bolivia (Republic of)
CQA-CUZ	Portugal
CVA-CXZ	Uruguay (Eastern Republic of)
CYA-CZZ	Canada
C2A-C2Z	Nauru (Republic of)
C3A-C3Z	Andorra (Principality of)
C4A-C4Z	Cyprus (Republic of)
C5A-C5Z	Gambia (Republic of the)
C6A-C6Z	Bahamas (Commonwealth of the)
C7A-C7Z	World Meteorological Organization
C8A-C9Z	Mozambique (Republic of)
DAA-DRZ	Germany (Federal Republic of)
DSA-DTZ	Korea (Republic of)
DUA-DZZ	Philippines (Republic of the)
D2A-D3Z	Angola (Republic of)
D4A-D4Z	Cape Verde (Republic of)
D5A-D5Z	Liberia (Republic of)
D6A-D6Z	Comoros (Islamic Federal Republic of the)
D7A-D9Z	Korea (Republic of)
EAA-EHZ	Spain
EIA-EJZ	Ireland
EKA-EKZ	Armenia (Republic of)
ELA-ELZ	Liberia (Republic of)
EMA-EOZ	Ukraine
EPA-EQZ	Iran (Islamic Republic of)
ERA-ERZ	Moldova (Republic of)
ESA-ESZ	Estonia (Republic of)
ETA-ETZ	Ethiopia (Federal Democratic Republic of)
EUA-EWZ	Belarus (Republic of)

EXA-EXZ	Kyrgyz Republic
EYA-EYZ	Tajikistan (Republic of)
EZA-EZZ	Turkmenistan
E2A-E2Z	Thailand
E3A-E3Z	Eritrea
E4A-E4Z	Palestinian Authority
E5A-E5Z	New Zealand - Cook Islands (WRC-07)
E7A-E7Z	Bosnia and Herzegovina (Republic of) (WRC-07)
FAA-FZZ	France
GAA-GZZ	United Kingdom of Great Britain and Northern Ireland
HAA-HAZ	Hungary (Republic of)
HBA-HBZ	Switzerland (Confederation of)
HCA-HDZ	Ecuador
HEA-HEZ	Switzerland (Confederation of)
HFA-HFZ	Poland (Republic of)
HGA-HGZ	Hungary (Republic of)
HHA-HHZ	Haiti (Republic of)
HIA-HIZ	Dominican Republic
HJA-HKZ	Colombia (Republic of)
HLA-HLZ	Korea (Republic of)
HMA-HMZ	Democratic People's Republic of Korea
HNA-HNZ	Iraq (Republic of)
HOA-HPZ	Panama (Republic of)
HQA-HRZ	Honduras (Republic of)
HSA-HSZ	Thailand
HTA-HTZ	Nicaragua
HUA-HUZ	El Salvador (Republic of)
HVA-HVZ	Vatican City State
HWA-HYZ	France
HZA-HZZ	Saudi Arabia (Kingdom of)
H2A-H2Z	Cyprus (Republic of)
H3A-H3Z	Panama (Republic of)
H4A-H4Z	Solomon Islands
H6A-H7Z	Nicaragua
H8A-H9Z	Panama (Republic of)
IAA-IZZ	Italy
JAA-JSZ	Japan
JTA-JVZ	Mongolia
JWA-JXZ	Norway
JYA-JYZ	Jordan (Hashemite Kingdom of)
JZA-JZZ	Indonesia (Republic of)
J2A-J2Z	Djibouti (Republic of)
J3A-J3Z	Grenada
J4A-J4Z	Greece
J5A-J5Z	Guinea-Bissau (Republic of)

J6A-J6Z	Saint Lucia
J7A-J7Z	Dominica (Commonwealth of)
J8A-J8Z	Saint Vincent and the Grenadines
KAA-KZZ	**United States of America**
LAA-LNZ	Norway
LOA-LWZ	Argentine Republic
LXA-LXZ	Luxembourg
LYA-LYZ	Lithuania (Republic of)
LZA-LZZ	Bulgaria (Republic of)
L2A-L9Z	Argentine Republic
MAA-MZZ	United Kingdom of Great Britain and Northern Ireland
NAA-NZZ	**United States of America**
OAA-OCZ	Peru
ODA-ODZ	Lebanon
OEA-OEZ	Austria
OFA-OJZ	Finland
OKA-OLZ	Czech Republic
OMA-OMZ	Slovak Republic
ONA-OTZ	Belgium
OUA-OZZ	Denmark
PAA-PIZ	Netherlands (Kingdom of the)
PJA-PJZ	Netherlands (Kingdom of the) - Netherlands Antilles
PKA-POZ	Indonesia (Republic of)
PPA-PYZ	Brazil (Federative Republic of)
PZA-PZZ	Suriname (Republic of)
P2A-P2Z	Papua New Guinea
P3A-P3Z	Cyprus (Republic of)
P4A-P4Z	Netherlands (Kingdom of the) - Aruba
P5A-P9Z	Democratic People's Republic of Korea
RAA-RZZ	Russian Federation
SAA-SMZ	Sweden
SNA-SRZ	Poland (Republic of)
SSA-SSM	Egypt (Arab Republic of)
SSN-STZ	Sudan (Republic of the)
SUA-SUZ	Egypt (Arab Republic of)
SVA-SZZ	Greece
S2A-S3Z	Bangladesh (People's Republic of)
S5A-S5Z	Slovenia (Republic of)
S6A-S6Z	Singapore (Republic of)
S7A-S7Z	Seychelles (Republic of)
S8A-S8Z	South Africa (Republic of)
S9A-S9Z	Sao Tome and Principe (Democratic Republic of)
TAA-TCZ	Turkey
TDA-TDZ	Guatemala (Republic of)
TEA-TEZ	Costa Rica

TFA-TFZ	Iceland
TGA-TGZ	Guatemala (Republic of)
THA-THZ	France
TIA-TIZ	Costa Rica
TJA-TJZ	Cameroon (Republic of)
TKA-TKZ	France
TLA-TLZ	Central African Republic
TMA-TMZ	France
TNA-TNZ	Congo (Republic of the)
TOA-TQZ	France
TRA-TRZ	Gabonese Republic
TSA-TSZ	Tunisia
TTA-TTZ	Chad (Republic of)
TUA-TUZ	Côte d'Ivoire (Republic of)
TVA-TXZ	France
TYA-TYZ	Benin (Republic of)
TZA-TZZ	Mali (Republic of)
T2A-T2Z	Tuvalu
T3A-T3Z	Kiribati (Republic of)
T4A-T4Z	Cuba
T5A-T5Z	Somali Democratic Republic
T6A-T6Z	Afghanistan (Islamic State of)
T7A-T7Z	San Marino (Republic of)
T8A-T8Z	Palau (Republic of)
UAA-UIZ	Russian Federation
UJA-UMZ	Uzbekistan (Republic of)
UNA-UQZ	Kazakhstan (Republic of)
URA-UZZ	Ukraine
VAA-VGZ	Canada
VHA-VNZ	Australia
VOA-VOZ	Canada
VPA-VQZ	United Kingdom of Great Britain and Northern Ireland
VRA-VRZ	China (People's Republic of) - Hong Kong
VSA-VSZ	United Kingdom of Great Britain and Northern Ireland
VTA-VWZ	India (Republic of)
VXA-VYZ	Canada
VZA-VZZ	Australia
V2A-V2Z	Antigua and Barbuda
V3A-V3Z	Belize
V4A-V4Z	Saint Kitts and Nevis
V5A-V5Z	Namibia (Republic of)
V6A-V6Z	Micronesia (Federated States of)
V7A-V7Z	Marshall Islands (Republic of the)
V8A-V8Z	Brunei Darussalam
WAA-WZZ	**United States of America**

XAA-XIZ	Mexico
XJA-XOZ	Canada
XPA-XPZ	Denmark
XQA-XRZ	Chile
XSA-XSZ	China (People's Republic of)
XTA-XTZ	Burkina Faso
XUA-XUZ	Cambodia (Kingdom of)
XVA-XVZ	Viet Nam (Socialist Republic of)
XWA-XWZ	Lao People's Democratic Republic
XXA-XXZ	China (People's Republic of) - Macao (WRC-07)
XYA-XZZ	Myanmar (Union of)
YAA-YAZ	Afghanistan (Islamic State of)
YBA-YHZ	Indonesia (Republic of)
YIA-YIZ	Iraq (Republic of)
YJA-YJZ	Vanuatu (Republic of)
YKA-YKZ	Syrian Arab Republic
YLA-YLZ	Latvia (Republic of)
YMA-YMZ	Turkey
YNA-YNZ	Nicaragua
YOA-YRZ	Romania
YSA-YSZ	El Salvador (Republic of)
YTA-YUZ	Serbia (Republic of) (WRC-07)
YVA-YYZ	Venezuela (Republic of)
Y2A-Y9Z	Germany (Federal Republic of)
ZAA-ZAZ	Albania (Republic of)
ZBA-ZJZ	United Kingdom of Great Britain and Northern Ireland
ZKA-ZMZ	New Zealand
ZNA-ZOZ	United Kingdom of Great Britain and Northern Ireland
ZPA-ZPZ	Paraguay (Republic of)
ZQA-ZQZ	United Kingdom of Great Britain and Northern Ireland
ZRA-ZUZ	South Africa (Republic of)
ZVA-ZZZ	Brazil (Federative Republic of)
Z2A-Z2Z	Zimbabwe (Republic of)
Z3A-Z3Z	The Former Yugoslav Republic of Macedonia
2AA-2ZZ	United Kingdom of Great Britain and Northern Ireland
3AA-3AZ	Monaco (Principality of)
3BA-3BZ	Mauritius (Republic of)
3CA-3CZ	Equatorial Guinea (Republic of)
3DA-3DM	Swaziland (Kingdom of)
3DN-3DZ	Fiji (Republic of)
3EA-3FZ	Panama (Republic of)
3GA-3GZ	Chile
3HA-3UZ	China (People's Republic of)
3VA-3VZ	Tunisia
3WA-3WZ	Viet Nam (Socialist Republic of)

3XA-3XZ	Guinea (Republic of)
3YA-3YZ	Norway
3ZA-3ZZ	Poland (Republic of)
4AA-4CZ	Mexico
4DA-4IZ	Philippines (Republic of the)
4JA-4KZ	Azerbaijani Republic
4LA-4LZ	Georgia (Republic of)
4MA-4MZ	Venezuela (Republic of)
4OA-4OZ	Montenegro (Republic of) (WRC-07)
4PA-4SZ	Sri Lanka (Democratic Socialist Republic of)
4TA-4TZ	Peru
4UA-4UZ	United Nations
4VA-4VZ	Haiti (Republic of)
4WA-4WZ	Democratic Republic of Timor-Leste (WRC-03)
4XA-4XZ	Israel (State of)
4YA-4YZ	International Civil Aviation Organization
4ZA-4ZZ	Israel (State of)
5AA-5AZ	Libya (Socialist People's Libyan Arab Jamahiriya)
5BA-5BZ	Cyprus (Republic of)
5CA-5GZ	Morocco (Kingdom of)
5HA-5IZ	Tanzania (United Republic of)
5JA-5KZ	Colombia (Republic of)
5LA-5MZ	Liberia (Republic of)
5NA-5OZ	Nigeria (Federal Republic of)
5PA-5QZ	Denmark
5RA-5SZ	Madagascar (Republic of)
5TA-5TZ	Mauritania (Islamic Republic of)
5UA-5UZ	Niger (Republic of the)
5VA-5VZ	Togolese Republic
5WA-5WZ	Samoa (Independent State of)
5XA-5XZ	Uganda (Republic of)
5YA-5ZZ	Kenya (Republic of)
6AA-6BZ	Egypt (Arab Republic of)
6CA-6CZ	Syrian Arab Republic
6DA-6JZ	Mexico
6KA-6NZ	Korea (Republic of)
6OA-6OZ	Somali Democratic Republic
6PA-6SZ	Pakistan (Islamic Republic of)
6TA-6UZ	Sudan (Republic of the)
6VA-6WZ	Senegal (Republic of)
6XA-6XZ	Madagascar (Republic of)
6YA-6YZ	Jamaica
6ZA-6ZZ	Liberia (Republic of)
7AA-7IZ	Indonesia (Republic of)
7JA-7NZ	Japan

7OA-7OZ	Yemen (Republic of)
7PA-7PZ	Lesotho (Kingdom of)
7QA-7QZ	Malawi
7RA-7RZ	Algeria (People's Democratic Republic of)
7SA-7SZ	Sweden
7TA-7YZ	Algeria (People's Democratic Republic of)
7ZA-7ZZ	Saudi Arabia (Kingdom of)
8AA-8IZ	Indonesia (Republic of)
8JA-8NZ	Japan
8OA-8OZ	Botswana (Republic of)
8PA-8PZ	Barbados
8QA-8QZ	Maldives (Republic of)
8RA-8RZ	Guyana
8SA-8SZ	Sweden
8TA-8YZ	India (Republic of)
8ZA-8ZZ	Saudi Arabia (Kingdom of)
9AA-9AZ	Croatia (Republic of)
9BA-9DZ	Iran (Islamic Republic of)
9EA-9FZ	Ethiopia (Federal Democratic Republic of)
9GA-9GZ	Ghana
9HA-9HZ	Malta
9IA-9JZ	Zambia (Republic of)
9KA-9KZ	Kuwait (State of)
9LA-9LZ	Sierra Leone
9MA-9MZ	Malaysia
9NA-9NZ	Nepal
9OA-9TZ	Democratic Republic of the Congo
9UA-9UZ	Burundi (Republic of)
9VA-9VZ	Singapore (Republic of)
9WA-9WZ	Malaysia
9XA-9XZ	Rwandese Republic
9YA-9ZZ	Trinidad and Tobago

Third-Party Communications and Amateur Radio

If all of this information about ham radios is somewhat intimidating, do not despair. "You" can still use ham radios for communications without being a licensed operator. Yes, you do have to have a ham license in order to legally transmit by ham equipment (or be under the direct supervision of someone else who is licensed), but there is an alternative – third-party communication.

Third-party communications occur when a licensed operator sends either written or verbal messages on behalf of unlicensed persons or organizations. There are two "controls" on third-party communication.

First, the communication must be noncommercial and of a personal nature. Asking a ham operator to contact another ham operator located in an area just hit by tornados and, because of being without power, phones do not work in Grandma Sally's city so you can check up on her, is okay. Asking a ham to send a message out that you have an old Chevy for sale would not be okay.

Second, the message must be going to a permitted area. Transmitting from a US location to another US location is okay, but transmitting from the US to another country may not. Because third-party communications bypass a country's normal telephone and postal systems, many foreign governments forbid such communications. In order to transmit from one country to another, the other country must have signed a third-party agreement with the US. What follows is a list of those countries that do have third-party a communications agreement with the US.

V2	Antigua / Barbuda
LU	Argentina
VK	Australia
V3	Belize
CP	Bolivia
T9	Bosnia-Herzegovina
PY	Brazil
VE	Canada
CE	Chile
HK	Colombia
D6	Comoros (Federal Islamic Republic of)
TI	Costa Rica
CO	Cuba
HI	Dominican Republic
J7	Dominica
HC	Ecuador
YS	El Salvador
C5	Gambia, The
9G	Ghana
J3	Grenada
TG	Guatemala
8R	Guyana
HH	Haiti
HR	Honduras
4X	Israel
6Y	Jamaica
JY	Jordan
EL	Liberia
V7	Marshall Islands
XE	Mexico
V6	Micronesia, Federated States of

YN	Nicaragua
HP	Panama
ZP	Paraguay
OA	Peru
DU	Philippines
VR6	Pitcairn Island
V4	St. Christopher / Nevis
J6	St. Lucia
J8	St. Vincent and the Grenadines
9L	Sierra Leone
ZS	South Africa
3DA	Swaziland
9Y	Trinidad / Tobago
TA	Turkey
GB	United Kingdom
CX	Uruguay
YV	Venezuela
4U1ITUITU	Geneva
4U1VICVIC	Vienna

Remember, before TSHTF, keep your pantry well stocked, your powder dry, and your batteries fully charged. 73

APPENDIX A

American Radio Relay League

Affiliated Amateur Radio Clubs in

the District of Columbia

ARRL Affiliated Club   **George Washington University Amateur Radio Club**
City: Washington, DC
Call Sign: K3GWU
Section: MDC
Links: gwuarcars.org

ARRL Affiliated Club   **Voice of America Amateur Radio Club**
City: Washington, DC
Call Sign: K3VOA
Section: MDC
Links: www.k3voa.org

APPENDIX B

Amateur Radio License Holders

in

the District of Columbia

Call Sign: KB3GBK
Jon R Gribskov
134 10th St NE
Washington DC 20002

Call Sign: KB9WSW
Craig A Max IV
1522 10th St NW
Washington DC 200013214

Call Sign: KC2MUE
Shawn P Loveric
505 10th St SE
Washington DC 20003

Call Sign: KB3SEN
Michael Quattrone
116 11th St NE
Washington DC 20002

Call Sign: KB3LXO
Alan E Dixon
1904 11th St NW
Washington DC 20001

Call Sign: KB3LXN
Alison Simon
1904 11th St NW
Washington DC 20001

Call Sign: K3ZWV
Herbert T Gaskins
5206 11th St NE
Washington DC 20011

Call Sign: KC9UME
Nicholas A Rushizky
914 12th St NE
Washington DC 20002

Call Sign: N3YKY
Frederick A Browne
5213 12th St NE
Washington DC 200116413

Call Sign: KA3GOB
Gene A Gilstrap
5045 12th St NE
Washington DC 20017

Call Sign: KB3VZW
 Fcc Amateur Radio Club
445 12th St SW Rm 7-A802
Washington DC 20554

Call Sign: WA3FCC
 Fcc Amateur Radio Club
445 12th St SW Rm 7-A802
Washington DC 20554

Call Sign: KE4GLG
Darrell Duane
3110 13th St NW
Washington DC 200102408

Call Sign: KA1SLA
Stephen W Simpson
502 13th St SE
Washington DC 20003

Call Sign: KA3LEX
Ovid Marks
5112 13th St NW
Washington DC 20011

Call Sign: KB3CGP
Sunny L Raspet
1209 13th St NW Unit 207
Washington DC 20005

Call Sign: KB4DR
Frank J Feely III
146 13th St SE
Washington DC 20003

Call Sign: KC3XC
Mark A Wilcox
219 13th St SE
Washington DC 200031430

Call Sign: N3TEB
Norman A Sims
2529 14th St N E Apt 1
Washington DC 20018

Call Sign: KB3VAP
Ferdinando M Romano
4200 14th St NE
Washington DC 20017

Call Sign: N0NLY
John E Hoehn
2125 14th St NW Apt 909
Washington DC 20009

Call Sign: WA3MFH
Pierre A Finck
740 15th St NW
Washington DC 20005

Call Sign: W1OFZ
Joshua J Finnie
2325 15th St NW Apt 001
Washington DC 20009

Call Sign: AB3KG
Trammell Hudson
1527 16th NW 5
Washington DC 20036

Call Sign: KB3SPM
Salvadore P Motsuk
3420 16th St NW 202
Washington DC 200103013

Call Sign: AB3GP
Mark W Lukinovich
3636 16th St NW B-926
Washington DC 20010

Call Sign: W3HLY
Walter A Brester
4825 16th St NE
Washington DC 20017

Call Sign: KA3UIA
Charles H Fleischer
888 16th St NW
Washington DC 20006

Call Sign: W3EVZ
Denny A Newberry
3636 16th St NW
Washington DC 20010

Call Sign: KB2QPN
Michael A Weiss
2400 16th St NW 424
Washington DC 20009

Call Sign: KB3YCQ
John P Bishop
2480 16th St NW Apt 815
Washington DC 20009

Call Sign: WA3YQR
James E Davis
3636 16th St NW Apt Bg03
Washington DC 20010

Call Sign: W3NBC
Christian C O Brien
1514 17th St NW Apt B1
Washington DC 200093351

Call Sign: KA2GVN
Gilbert D Glass
3426 17th St NW
Washington DC 200101809

Call Sign: N3MYA
David G Rhodes
314 17th St SE
Washington DC 20002

Call Sign: N3CJW
Kenneth M Scheibel Sr
1325 18th St NW Apt 302
Washington DC 20036

Call Sign: W3AN
Dx Gang
1020 19th St   NW   Ste 880
Washington DC 20036

Call Sign: KD4RCI
Daniel J Wilhelm
1817 19th St NW
Washington DC 20009

Call Sign: KB3EMX
Karin B Assmann
1723 19th St NW
Washington DC 20009

Call Sign: WS6BR
Michael J Wilhelm
1817 19th St NW
Washington DC 20009

Call Sign: KA3SBU
James C Dickson
3203 19th St NW
Washington DC 20010

Call Sign: KE6QPB
Douglas J Bouley
2200 19th St NW 209
Washington DC 20009

Call Sign: KB3SKA
Troy A Mccurry
1025 1st St   SE 602
Washington DC 20003

Call Sign: KB3SXH
Anne Hopengarten
2206 1st St NW
Washington DC 20001

Call Sign: N4SZV
Michael D Nossaman
2333 20th NW
Washington DC 20009

Call Sign: KB1CJC
Aaron M Ucko
1301 20th St NW Apt 904
Washington DC 200366025

Call Sign: KA7DCX
Cheryl A England
532 20th St NW   109
Washington DC 20006

Call Sign: W3ETX
Ernest E Stephens Jr
4321 20th St NE
Washington DC 200183309

Call Sign: N9OKN
David K Barth
2407 20th St NW 98
Washington DC 20009

Call Sign: KB3BEN
Marcos Eguillor
1301 20th St NW Apt 407
Washington DC 20036

Call Sign: K0NB
Mark R Price
1400 20th St NW Apt 917
Washington DC 20036

Call Sign: KB3QOF
Clare E Rowland
510 21st St NW   608
Washington DC 20006

Call Sign: KB3QNX
Susannah Leahy
1099 22nd St NW Apt 1005
Washington DC 20037

Call Sign: N3TCD
John E Leake
3011 24th St NE
Washington DC 200182501

Call Sign: WA3WNL
James S Watts
3610 24th St NE
Washington DC 20018

Call Sign: KB3FFS
Karl A Pearson Sr
1851 24th St NE 204
Washington DC 20002

Call Sign: AA3XC
Karl A Pearson Sr
1851 24th St NE 204
Washington DC 20002

Call Sign: N3RHG
Sameer S Ramchandani
922 24ths T NW Apt 214
Washington DC 20037

Call Sign: N1GBL
William I Eggleston
940 25th St NW
Washington DC 20037

Call Sign: N3WCN
Daniel M Laurent
950 25th St NW Apt 419N
Washington DC 20037

Call Sign: KA1SQC
Jane W Eggleston
950 25th St NW Apt 1025
Washington DC 20037

Call Sign: KB3FZD
John R Mcguire
5743 26th St NW
Washington DC 200151113

Call Sign: KB3JGZ
Jennifer L Jenkins
955 26th St NW Apt 208
Washington DC 20037

Call Sign: KA2RBH
Alan C Levine
4701 29th Pl NW
Washington DC 20008

Call Sign: N3ES
Earl F Skelton
6311 29th Pl NW
Washington DC 20015

Call Sign: KA3TOE
David L Feldman
4455 29th St NW
Washington DC 20008

Call Sign: KA1SFI
Stephen R Gough
2745 29th St NW 619
Washington DC 20008

Call Sign: WF3Q
John E Holloway
5431 30th Pl NW
Washington DC 20015

Call Sign: K3JEH
John E Holloway
5431 30th Pl NW
Washington DC 20015

Call Sign: N3UT
Gregory M Jones
6612 31st Pl NW
Washington DC 20015

Call Sign: KA3WPT
Geoffrey M Alprin
6604 31st St NW
Washington DC 20015

Call Sign: KA3EHH
Jonathan Silverstone
6633 32nd Pl NW
Washington DC 20015

Call Sign: N1VTN
Edson W Pereira
6686 32nd St NW
Washington DC 20015

Call Sign: KB3DX
Jeffrey Blumenfeld
6614 32nd St NW
Washington DC 20015

Call Sign: AB3LD
Joseph S Piacentini
5612 33rd St NW
Washington DC 20015

Call Sign: KB3HPK
Robert D Kovach
6946 33rd St NW
Washington DC 200151406

Call Sign: KB3PHO
Sasha Strickland
1523 34th St NW
Washington DC 20007

Call Sign: KB3MKB
Brian A Lockett
3109 34th St NW
Washington DC 20008

Call Sign: KB3MKA
Danuta E Lockett
3109 34th St NW
Washington DC 20008

Call Sign: KB3EKQ
Laertes Gillis Jr
1210 34th St SE
Washington DC 20019

Call Sign: WA3DAR
Robert H Mead
2326 37th St NW
Washington DC 20007

Call Sign: N3CHH
David S Reed
3401 38th St NW Apt 227
Washington DC 20016

Call Sign: WB3AMN
Robert P Dickey
1647 38th St SE
Washington DC 20020

Call Sign: N3BKJ
Frederick B Hendricks
2209 39th St NW
Washington DC 20007

Call Sign: KA3NYH
Peter R Kolker
5524 39th St NW
Washington DC 20015

Call Sign: KA3TNG
David C Arpee
3810 39th St NW A121
Washington DC 20016

Call Sign: KF4LLR
Mark E Driscoll
4302 3rd St NW
Washington DC 20011

Call Sign: WB3CQI
Douglas Thomas Jr
6415 3rd St NW
Washington DC 20012

Call Sign: KB3OHV
Lance S Benson
18 3rd St SE
Washington DC 20003

Call Sign: AB2QE
Noele P Nelson
2331 40th St   2
Washington DC 20007

Call Sign: KG6CWD
Dotan Halevy
2331 40th St NW 2
Washington DC 20007

Call Sign: AE6CF
Itzhak Halevy
2331 40th St NW 2
Washington DC 20007

Call Sign: N3OXL
Gilbert S Edwards
5035 41st St NW
Washington DC 20016

Call Sign: NM3D
Zane A Lang
2400 41st St NW 305
Washington DC 20007

Call Sign: N5AKH
David C Straw
5325 42nd Pl NW
Washington DC 20015

Call Sign: W3STR
George J Tedore
5010 42nd St NW
Washington DC 20016

Call Sign: KB3ASU
Barbara J Euser
3009 45th St NW
Washington DC 20016

Call Sign: K3DRA
Arnold L Polinger
3015 45th St NW
Washington DC 20016

Call Sign: W3IIC
Mahlon H Norton
4436 45th St NW
Washington DC 20016

Call Sign: KB3KEV
Mark D Heckendorn
4516 45th St NW
Washington DC 20016

Call Sign: N3QQB
Joseph B D Angelo
4713 45th St NW
Washington DC 20016

Call Sign: KB3CXI
Richard F Reed
4816 46th NW
Washington DC 20016

Call Sign: WA3NPO
Frederick C Hillyard Sr
4222 47th St NW
Washington DC 20016

Call Sign: NN3G
John A Mc Carthy Jr
4819 47th St NW
Washington DC 20016

Call Sign: KB3POH
Gleb V Drobkov
2234 48th St NW
Washington DC 20007

Call Sign: KB3TOH
David M Nolton Jr
443 4th St NE
Washington DC 20002

Call Sign: KJ4BQR
Jason W Trautman
811 4th St NW 1207
Washington DC 20001

Call Sign: K4JWT
Jason W Trautman
811 4th St NW 1207
Washington DC 20001

Call Sign: W1ITV
Terry W Tuttle
1362 4th St SW
Washington DC 20024

Call Sign: KA3TKF
Leopold Luschnitz
15 4th St NE
Washington DC 20002

Call Sign: KB3NVU
Nicole K Warner
601 4th St NW
Washington DC 20013

Call Sign: KB3PMC
Eric S Mendelsohn
6827 4th St NW Apt 309
Washington DC 20012

Call Sign: WA2EFZ
Charles G Rogoff
110 4th St SE
Washington DC 20003

Call Sign: W3HQ
Edward Ramos
603 4th St SW
Washington DC 20024

Call Sign: N3JSX
Faye M Bullock
1435 4th St SW B316
Washington DC 20024

Call Sign: KB3SOA
Garner Marshall
117 53rd St NE
Washington DC 20019

Call Sign: KB3RGW
Megan L Mccarty
212 5th St NE
Washington DC 20002

Call Sign: KC7LGZ
Daniel B Whiting
101 5th St NE
Washington DC 20002

Call Sign: N3PGT
Douglas J Alspach
123 5th St NE
Washington DC 20002

Call Sign: KC9NZI
Samuel W Blevins
1111 5th St NW
Washington DC 20001

Call Sign: WA3BDS
Sidney C Montgomery
6518 5th St NW
Washington DC 20012

Call Sign: KD5EZK
Wiley P Rittenhouse
770 5th St NW Apt 1202
Washington DC 20001

Call Sign: KF6TKQ
Joseph C Pope
211 5th St SE
Washington DC 20003

Call Sign: WC6Z
Franz A Delahan
537 5th St SE
Washington DC 20003

Call Sign: K3WE
Walter G Egan Jr
312 6th St NE
Washington DC 20002

Call Sign: KB3NZG
James W Avery
611 6th Pl SW
Washington DC 20024

Call Sign: N3YQF
David M Smith
120 6th St NE
Washington DC 20002

Call Sign: KB3ALM
Hidan O Ricco
831 6th St SW
Washington DC 20024

Call Sign: N3RFE
Steven C Kinsley
26 7th St NE
Washington DC 20002

Call Sign: KB3MS
Alonzo York
6030 8th NW
Washington DC 20011

Call Sign: KA3WVI
Delores M Rushing
4303 9th St NW
Washington DC 20011

Call Sign: KB3IJV
Jason Snell
641 A St NE
Washington DC 200026029

Call Sign: K3ASM
Jason Snell
641 A St NE
Washington DC 200026029

Call Sign: KB3WAG
Roy Roberts
1337 A St NE
Washington DC 20002

Call Sign: AE0NS
Roy Roberts
1337 A St NE
Washington DC 20002

Call Sign: KB3FQQ
John M Atkisson
820 A St SE
Washington DC 20003

Call Sign: KA3TMG
Kevin C Wells
1615 A St SE
Washington DC 20003

Call Sign: WA3OID
Roland L Butler
3344 Alabama Ave SE
Washington DC 200201463

Call Sign: N3NXI
Gustine B Phifer
4620 Alabama Ave SE
Washington DC 20019

Call Sign: N3YSR
Philippe M Carlier
4533 Albemarle St
Washington DC 20016

Call Sign: W4IIA
William T Mc Aninch
3010 Albemarle St NW
Washington DC 20008

Call Sign: KB3MRB
Rodger L Currie
4704 Albemarle St NW
Washington DC 20016

Call Sign: WB2PWC
Ronald B Sann
3644 Alton Pl NW
Washington DC 200084220

Call Sign: N3HFR
Robert L Mitchell
3920 Ames St NE
Washington DC 20019

Call Sign: N3OZM
Mark J Helm
0 Andrews Cir
Washington DC 20032

Call Sign: KB3CST
Rodrigo De Los Rios
2802 Arizona Ave NW
Washington DC 20016

Call Sign: N3GWJ
Jean Michel Houde
2802 Arizona Ave NW
Washington DC 20016

Call Sign: N3NGI
Jean Franco Hovde
2802 Arizona Ave NW
Washington DC 20016

Call Sign: N3XYQ
Roberto De Los Rios
2802 Arizona Ave NW
Washington DC 20016

Call Sign: N3XYR
Francois X Houde
2802 Arizona Ave NW
Washington DC 20016

Call Sign: KB3KKY
John K Gunther
2901 Arizona Ave NW
Washington DC 20016

Call Sign: KB3VPM
David V Halbeisen
4136 Arkansas Ave NW
Washington DC 20011

Call Sign: KD4CNX
William W Schmitt
209 Ascot Pl NE
Washington DC 20002

Call Sign: N3JAV
Bill Adler
3409 Ashley Ter NW
Washington DC 200083239

Call Sign: W3OXY
Daniel L Bradford
301 Atlantic St SE
Washington DC 20032

Call Sign: KB3REJ
Reagan E-Star Group
1 Aviation Cir   Ma 630
Washington DC 20001

Call Sign: K3CSU
Reagan E-Star Group
1 Aviation Cir   Ma 630
Washington DC 20001

Call Sign: KB3NDQ
National E-Star Group
1 Aviation Dr Ma 610   Hangar 5
Washington DC 20001

Call Sign: K4DCA
National E-Star Group
1 Aviation Dr Ma 610 Hangar 5
Washington DC 20001

Call Sign: KB2BOB
Laurence B Balter
3293 B Sutton Pl NW
Washington DC 20016

Call Sign: WA3RNJ
Richard B Mc Mahill
3624 Bangor St SE
Washington DC 20020

Call Sign: NV3Z
Michael G Katzmann
6654 Barnaby St NW
Washington DC 20015

Call Sign: WB3FME
Mark D Rhoads
0 Beekman Pl NW
Washington DC 200094080

Call Sign: KB3USG
Paul A Kennedy
2032 Belmont Rd NW 518
Washington DC 20009

Call Sign: KB3HXH
Edward W Pinkard
1807 Belmont Rd Apt 207
Washington DC 20009

Call Sign: N3REX
Tobias J Halliday
5024 Belt Road NW
Washington DC 20016

Call Sign: WA6MZJ
Matthew J Brazil
4015 Benton St NW Apt 3
Washington DC 20007

Call Sign: K2ACX
Brian D Cahill
1832 Biltmore St NW Apt 46
Washington DC 20009

Call Sign: W3ODE
Joseph R Fletcher
7225 Blair Rd NW
Washington DC 20012

Call Sign: N3AZF
Forrest L Headley
2201 Branch Ave
Washington DC 20020

Call Sign: KK4AF
George M Bedinger
4701 Brandywine St NW
Washington DC 20016

Call Sign: N3KIT
John L Ryan II
134 Bryant St NW
Washington DC 20001

Call Sign: KE5DBY
Bernard J Roulston
227 Burwell St
Bolling AFB DC 20032

Call Sign: KB3KII
Richard H Lamb
4425 Butterworth Pl NW
Washington DC 20016

Call Sign: AA3WQ
Thomas A Cotton
4429 Butterworth Pl NW
Washington DC 20016

Call Sign: K5TWO
Thomas A Cotton
4429 Butterworth Pl NW
Washington DC 20016

Call Sign: W3HQU
Henry C Lybrand
4201 Butterworth Pl NW Apt 327
Washington DC 20016

Call Sign: KD4HJ
David R Zorich
1588 C Eglin Way
Bolling AFB DC 20032

Call Sign: W2SKE
William A Leonard
2411 California St
Washington DC 20008

Call Sign: KB3GBI
Ayaanah Bilaal
5115 Call Pl SE
Washington DC 20019

Call Sign: KB3GBM
Maryam L Bilaal - Smith
5115 Call Pl SE
Washington DC 20019

Call Sign: KB3FYW
Addison E Smith
5115 Call Pl SE
Washington DC 20019

Call Sign: WB2WBA
Robin B Martin
2700 Calvert St NW
Washington DC 20008

Call Sign: KB8ZKO
John T Ohm
2701 Calvert St NW Apt 715
Washington DC 200082624

Call Sign: KB3HJK
Kevin E Shepherd
2701 Calvert St NW 203
Washington DC 20008

Call Sign: KG6EFT
James A Scott
2701 Calvert St NW Apt 821
Washington DC 20008

Call Sign: N7VVC
Nicholas G Retson
4201 Cathedral Ave NW   1220E
Washington DC 20016

Call Sign: WA3MBE
Harold J Kerr
4201 Cathedral Ave NW
Washington DC 20016

Call Sign: KD5RYL
Matthew J Kelly
4201 Cathedral Ave NW Apt 1122E
Washington DC 20016

Call Sign: KA3EKU
Milton Freundel
4000 Cathedral Ave NW Apt 4B
Washington DC 20016

Call Sign: W1KSF
Norris J Ansell
4201 Cathedral Ave NW Apt 615 E
Washington DC 20016

Call Sign: W2EE
Mortimer Rogoff
4201 Cathedral Ave NW Apt 914W
Washington DC 200164966

Call Sign: K8SIQ
Thomas K Mcknight
2236 Cathedral Avenue
Washington DC 20008

Call Sign: KA3JPE
La Conte O Saunders
5527 Central Ave SE
Washington DC 20019

Call Sign: KB3UYD
Sean Jaeger
3163 Chandler St SW
Washington DC 20032

Call Sign: N3QEX
Harold E Lawrence Sr
3100 Cherry Rd NE
Washington DC 20018

Call Sign: WA4HQD
William L Menard
3223 Chesapeake St NW
Washington DC 20008

Call Sign: K3QFG
Philip W Wirtz
3624 Chesapeake St NW
Washington DC 20008

Call Sign: KA3OXI
David A Schechter
4620 Chesapeake St NW
Washington DC 20016

Call Sign: N3TFK
Stephen L Babcock
3041 Chestnut St NW
Washington DC 20015

Call Sign: W2NJS
Thomas W Donohoe
3057 Chestnut St NW
Washington DC 20015

Call Sign: KA3YZM
Peter Basch
5824 Chevy Chase Pky NW
Washington DC 20015

Call Sign: KD3A
Raymond J Lustig Jr
4509 Clark Pl NW
Washington DC 200072502

Call Sign: KB2ROJ
Benjamin J Montalbano
3209 Cleveland Ave NW
Washington DC 20008

Call Sign: KB3EJN
Eleanor R Whitley
5224 Cloud Pl NE
Washington DC 20019

Call Sign: KB3VPZ
Andrew Patriss
1820 Clydesdale Pl NW 112
Washington DC 20009

Call Sign: N3JGL
David A Drysdale
589 Columbia Rd NW 10
Washington DC 20001

Call Sign: KB3RVQ
Elliot D Williams
1851 Columbia Rd NW Apt 407
Washington DC 20009

Call Sign: KB3TKJ
Arjun B Prasad
1868 Columbia Rd NW Apt 711
Washington DC 20009

Call Sign: KB2MMF
Marc G Strass
3801 Conn Ave Apt 723
Washington DC 20008

Call Sign: K3HBZ
Harold J Thompson
4801 Conn Ave NW
Washington DC 20008

Call Sign: WB3KTI
Frank E Bowman
4545 Conn Ave NW Apt 925
Washington DC 20008

Call Sign: N3GA
Masato Suzuki
1130 Connecticut Ave   NW   Ste 1100
Washington DC 20036

Call Sign: KC5UJY
David M Hall
2929 Connecticut Ave   NW Apt   407
Washington DC 20008

Call Sign: W3ULS
John S Rippey
4740 Connecticut Ave NW   1003
Washington DC 20008

Call Sign: N4HOO
Stephen M Saff
4707 Connecticut Ave 210
Washington DC 20008

Call Sign: KB3MQY
Michael T Goodrum
3801 Connecticut Ave Apt 212
Washington DC 20008

Call Sign: KB3SXV
Matthew J Hoffman
2726 Connecticut Ave Apt 403
Washington DC 20008

Call Sign: K3PJI
Donald H Robbins
2852 Connecticut Ave NW
Washington DC 20008

Call Sign: KB3DQD
Michael K Edler
4607 Connecticut Ave NW
Washington DC 20008

Call Sign: KB3LVG
Mark I Uretsky
3133 Connecticut Ave NW   Apt 723
Washington DC 20008

Call Sign: WB9JHW
Morris M Hornik
4850 Connecticut Ave NW   1006
Washington DC 200085908

Call Sign: KB3OSC
Frank T Winstead
4545 Connecticut Ave NW   508
Washington DC 20008

Call Sign: N2SOK
Tomas A Bonome
4601 Connecticut Ave NW   106
Washington DC 20008

Call Sign: KB3YFL
Christian J Shuler
5112 Connecticut Ave NW   111
Washington DC 20008

Call Sign: KB3VGR
David A Ziembicki Jr
5410 Connecticut Ave NW   302
Washington DC 20015

Call Sign: AB3IU
Claudio P Leite
2929 Connecticut Ave NW   710
Washington DC 200081400

Call Sign: WB8EOB
Ronald H Clark
2101 Connecticut Ave NW 24
Washington DC 20008

Call Sign: KK6SQ
Michael G Le Desma
2828 Connecticut Ave NW 814
Washington DC 20008

Call Sign: KB3BBE
Edgar Z Steever Jr
3000 Connecticut Ave NW Apt 124
Washington DC 20008

Call Sign: N3KGM
Quinton N Marsh
4901 Connecticut Ave NW Apt 210
Washington DC 20008

Call Sign: KB3MTE
Deborah J Carlos
3801 Connecticut Ave NW Apt 212
Washington DC 20008

Call Sign: KC9PEJ
Susan J Schaefer
4500 Connecticut Ave NW Apt 305
Washington DC 20008

Call Sign: KB3IHK
Masato Suzuki
1130 Connecticut Ave NW Ste 1100
Washington DC 200363904

Call Sign: KC7KAP
Scott W Geibel
4301 Connecticut Ave NW Ste 280
Washington DC 20008

Call Sign: AB2RZ
Rudolf W Burgi
4501 Connecticut Avenue NW
Washington DC 20008

Call Sign: KB3GAO
 Department Of Commerce Amateur Radio
Society
1401 Constitution Ave NW Rm 4624
Washington DC 20230

Call Sign: W4UOO
Kenneth Wise
507 D St SE
Washington DC 20003

Call Sign: KB9ZNF
Thomas C Clancy III
1009 D St SE
Washington DC 20003

Call Sign: AA3CD
James R Coleman
1013 Decatur St NE
Washington DC 20017

Call Sign: NJ3Q
Willie L Rutherford
721 Delafield St NE
Washington DC 20017

Call Sign: WB4GZD
William W Layton
1311 Delaware Ave SW
Washington DC 20024

Call Sign: N3SBM
Ronald A Fenwick
325 Delifield Pl Apt 1 NW
Washington DC 20011

Call Sign: WB3JML
Jeffrey R Swegel
95 Duncan Ave Ste A
Bolling AFB DC 20032

Call Sign: K3EVF
R Brooke Bortner
631 E Capitol St   SE
Washington DC 20003

Call Sign: WA2TIU
Terence R Bertele
804 E Capitol St NE
Washington DC 20003

Call Sign: KB3FFW
Peggy R Godfrey
5901 E Capt St SE 1212
Washington DC 20019

Call Sign: KB3YFP
Adwait Kocharekar
2301 E St NW Apt A914
Washington DC 20037

Call Sign: WB2BBS
Dennis J Dunbar
35 E St   NW
Washington DC 20001

Call Sign: W3UW
Gregory D Poe
675 E St NW Apt 310
Washington DC 20004

Call Sign: N3EZE
Terry L Claassen
228 E St NE
Washington DC 20002

Call Sign: KC2YQJ
Dinesh Cyanam
2301 E St NW Apt A914
Washington DC 20037

Call Sign: KB3YGP
George Washington University Amateur
Radio Club And Research Station
2301 E St NW Apt A914
Washington DC 20037

Call Sign: AB3DC
Dinesh Cyanam
2301 E St NW Apt A914
Washington DC 20037

Call Sign: KF5HDS
Sanjay Srikanth Nekkanti
2301 E St NW Apt A914
Washington DC 20037

Call Sign: AB3OE
Sanjay Srikanth Nekkanti
2301 E St NW Apt A914
Washington DC 20037

Call Sign: N0TFQ
Bill Western
601 E St NW B3 181
Washington DC 200490001

Call Sign: WB3KIC
Weaver A Shepperson
149 E St SE
Washington DC 20003

Call Sign: KB3CLL
Christina D Briseno
1364 E St SE 2
Washington DC 20003

Call Sign: WB0FRD
Frank H Wonschik Jr
117 E St SE 102
Washington DC 20003

Call Sign: AA3KZ
Tyrone Harris
5602 Eastern Ave NEast

Washington DC 20011

Call Sign: N3TFJ
William D Coleman
6610 Eastern Ave NW
Washington DC 20012

Call Sign: W2BOY
Robert H Kupperman
2832 Ellicott St NW
Washington DC 20008

Call Sign: N3PWQ
Constantine M Seremetis
4434 Ellicott St NW
Washington DC 20016

Call Sign: KC3LI
Robert V Maudlin
2906 Ellicott Terrace NW
Washington DC 200081023

Call Sign: KB1HAH
Ross B Schulman
1422 Euclid St NW
Washington DC 20009

Call Sign: WA3HMO
Marc L Zell
1725 Eye St NW Ste 300
Washington DC 20006

Call Sign: W6OO
Akihiko Ikeura
2030 F St NW Apt 402
Washington DC 200064241

Call Sign: N3ZTH
Janet R Gregor
651 F St NE
Washington DC 20002

Call Sign: WA3WRN
Joseph A Gregor
651 F St NE

Washington DC 20002

Washington DC 20011

Call Sign: W3WWW
Sylvester R Smith III
661 F St NE
Washington DC 20002

Call Sign: KB3GOP
Kathryn A Taylor
7900 Frankfurt Pl   Cons
Washington DC 205217900

Call Sign: W4ZDU
Russell Smith III
661 F St NE
Washington DC 20002

Call Sign: W3EIL
Chester R Martin
1719 Franklin St NE
Washington DC 20018

Call Sign: KA3BJU
Dorothy E Foster
1252 Farragut Pl NE
Washington DC 20017

Call Sign: N3DTZ
Harold W Hammock
1317 Ft Stevens Dr NW
Washington DC 20011

Call Sign: WB3DCK
Jonathan Foster
1252 Farragut Pl NE
Washington DC 20017

Call Sign: W3DXO
J Robert F Falabella
4606 Ft Totten Dr NE
Washington DC 20011

Call Sign: WA2HDD
Jonathan B Bender
4411 Fessenden St   NW
Washington DC 200164065

Call Sign: KB3WKX
Hye-Min Choi
10 G St NE Ste 800
Washington DC 20002

Call Sign: N3UBK
Carl T Rowan Jr
2910 Fessenden St NW
Washington DC 20008

Call Sign: KB3WKY
Ji-In Seok
10 G St NE Ste 800
Washington DC 20002

Call Sign: KF4UAS
Lawrence A Calabro
4052 Fessenden St NW
Washington DC 20016

Call Sign: KB3QNY
William J Fagan
815 G St SW
Washington DC 20024

Call Sign: K3GU
 Gallaudet University Amateur Radio Club
800 Florida Avenue NE
Washington DC 200023695

Call Sign: KA3WVH
James M Giordano
0 G St SW
Washington DC 20024

Call Sign: K3DB
Joseph F Falabella
4606 Fort Totten Dr NE

Call Sign: W3CL
Carl P Lagoda
103 G St SW Apt 813B

Washington DC 20024

Call Sign: N3HFQ
George R Reed
246 Gallatin St NW
Washington DC 20011

Call Sign: KB3JQS
Kevin L Westberg
101 Garrison St SW
Bolling AFB DC 20032

Call Sign: WA3HBE
Paul A Ritacco
3962 Georgetown Ct NW
Washington DC 20007

Call Sign: W3HBK
Carl H Bergman
1301 Geranium St NW
Washington DC 20012

Call Sign: N3DYQ
Eric E Meyer
1303 Geranium St NW
Washington DC 20012

Call Sign: AA3ZW
Eric E Meyer
1303 Geranium St NW
Washington DC 20012

Call Sign: NN3B
Eric E Meyer
1303 Geranium St NW
Washington DC 20012

Call Sign: KF4JZS
Felipe Hernandez
780 Girard St NW
Washington DC 20001

Call Sign: WA3HPS
Calvin J Cooley
4020 Grant St NE

Washington DC 20019

Call Sign: KC7UAL
Rolf Muenter
4452 Greenwich Parkway
Washington DC 20007

Call Sign: N3BPO
Elliod Dent
4322 H St SE
Washington DC 20019

Call Sign: KB3FEA
William A Gilliam
606 Hamilton St NW
Washington DC 20011

Call Sign: KE3PA
James L Moseley
711 Hamlin NE Apt 1
Washington DC 20017

Call Sign: KD3AE
Stephen J Rosenman
3911 Harrison St NW
Washington DC 20015

Call Sign: N3ZYO
Joseph E Mallet
3703 Harrison St NW
Washington DC 20015

Call Sign: WB3ENI
Eugene J Markus
4428 Harrison St NW
Washington DC 20015

Call Sign: KB3NJH
Patricia C Anderson
1476 Harvard St
Washington DC 20009

Call Sign: KB3GOO
Thomas J Lacy
3200 Havana Pl

Washington DC 205213200

Call Sign: W3GUG
Stephen A Becker
4029 Highwood Ct NW
Washington DC 20007

Call Sign: N3ZGN
Ismael Gonzalez
3435 Holmead Pl NW 409
Washington DC 20010

Call Sign: K3HFF
Stephen A Miller
6214 Hope Dr
Washington DC 20031

Call Sign: N3LYS
Thomas C Green
3738 Huntington St NW
Washington DC 20015

Call Sign: KB3LXM
James K Hall
804 I St NE
Washington DC 20002

Call Sign: W3EVB
Stanley J Dlugosz
2515 I St NW
Washington DC 20037

Call Sign: KB3JAC
Rodney M Jones
201 I St SW Apt 139
Washington DC 200244229

Call Sign: N8HM
Paul R Stoetzer
201 I St SW Apt V336
Washington DC 200244239

Call Sign: KA3DJN
Henry J Siano
3040 Idaho Ave NW 730

Washington DC 20016

Call Sign: KB3FFP
Will Tucker
4833 Illnois Ave NW
Washington DC 20011

Call Sign: WA2ETO
Jason F Isaacson
506 Independence Ave SE
Washington DC 20003

Call Sign: W3EUK
Edward B Dack
510 Independence Ave SE
Washington DC 20003

Call Sign: W3HYN
James R Wein
601 Independence Ave SE
Washington DC 20003

Call Sign: K3VOA
 Voice Of America Amateur Radio Club
330 Independence Ave SW Rm 2525 Croft
Washington DC 202370073

Call Sign: W3JTZ
Robert C Huey
3913 Ingomar St NW
Washington DC 20015

Call Sign: N3SOM
Raymond L Thompson
4620 Iowa Ave NW
Washington DC 20011

Call Sign: W3SEM
Clyde E Gurley
5018 Iowa Ave NW
Washington DC 20011

Call Sign: KB3YFQ
John E Jenifer
1241 Irving St NE

Washington DC 20017

Call Sign: KB3KI
Jackson L Davis Jr
1213 Jamaica St NE
Washington DC 200112722

Call Sign: W3OXH
Innes W Paxton
642 Jefferson St NE
Washington DC 20011

Call Sign: KB3RNG
Eoin F Fitzpatrick
231 Jefferson St NW
Washington DC 20011

Call Sign: WA3FMO
Luther D Miller Jr
3815 Jenifer St NW
Washington DC 20015

Call Sign: KB3MSZ
Wilson P Dizard III
4225 Jenifer St NW
Washington DC 20015

Call Sign: KC3CK
Mark E Siegel
3802 Jocelyn St NW
Washington DC 20015

Call Sign: KA3OHF
James D Diggs
114 Joliet St SW B
Washington DC 200321801

Call Sign: N3OYP
Kevin F Johnson
1333 Jonquil St NW
Washington DC 20012

Call Sign: W4LE
Michael S Benetato
1305 Juniper St

Washington DC 20012

Call Sign: KA3WVG
Robin L Gray Worrell
1424 Juniper St NW
Washington DC 20012

Call Sign: WM4W
Richard J Bodorff
1776 K St   NW   11th Floor
Washington DC 20006

Call Sign: N3QPK
Peter Martin
1301 K St NW
Washington DC 20005

Call Sign: W3QPL
Byron S Roudabush
3030 K St NW
Washington DC 20007

Call Sign: W3FQB
G Franklin Montgomery
2806 Kanawha St NW
Washington DC 20015

Call Sign: KA3YNQ
James P Beins
3812 Kanawha St NW
Washington DC 20015

Call Sign: KB3TVO
Marc S Smith
5735 Kansas Ave NW
Washington DC 20011

Call Sign: KB3RER
Don H Smith
3147 Kelly St
Bolling AFB DC 20032

Call Sign: KA3OYW
Rafael A Pena
740 Kenyon St   NW

Washington DC 20010

Washington DC 20032

Call Sign: NN3RP
Rafael A Pena
740 Kenyon St   NW
Washington DC 20010

Call Sign: N5GQD
Gary W Shipley
437 L'Enfant Plaza
Washington DC 20026

Call Sign: KB3CGH
Edwin M Velis Martinez
508 Kenyon St NW
Washington DC 20010

Call Sign: WD9DFJ
Steven J Crowley
614 Lexington Pl NE
Washington DC 20002

Call Sign: KB3TFS
Matthew R Wilkens
1800 Kilbourne Pl NW
Washington DC 20010

Call Sign: KC0KCN
James N Thames
625 Lexington Pl NE
Washington DC 20002

Call Sign: W3ICL
Ronald M Costell
3235 Klingle Rd NW
Washington DC 20008

Call Sign: W9NNZ
Theodore N Centala
2131 Lincoln Rd NE
Washington DC 20002

Call Sign: AJ2N
Hajime Kubo
1615 L St NW Ste 1215
Washington DC 20036

Call Sign: KB3RMJ
Claudio P Leite
1305 Linden Ct NE
Washington DC 200024429

Call Sign: N3MPQ
Richard T Wilkinson
0 Lackland Way
Bolling AFB DC 20336

Call Sign: KA3WZA
Jaromir Bauer
3900 Linneon Ave NW
Washington DC 20008

Call Sign: N3MCM
Renita A Holsendorff
1765 Lang Pl NE
Washington DC 20002

Call Sign: KB3BXI
Steven C Carson
1326 Longfellow St NW
Washington DC 20011

Call Sign: KB3HDL
Joseph W Easley
6701 Lazon Ave NW
Washington DC 20012

Call Sign: N3DKK
Albert J Forte Sr
5254 Loughboro Rd
Washington DC 20016

Call Sign: KB3OTC
John C Platt
448 Le Banm St SE

Call Sign: K3DBH
Robert I Dodge Jr
5080 Lowell St NW

Washington DC 200162616

Call Sign: N3RAI
Richard E Scott Jr
268 Luke Ave Box 952
Bolling AFB DC 20332

Call Sign: KB3IFV
David M Fratello
268 Luke Ave Box 1424
Bolling AFB DC 20332

Call Sign: KB3LDU
William J Dudley
420 Luray Pl NW
Washington DC 20010

Call Sign: N5RDR
Patricia Espinoza
490 M St SW W511
Washington DC 20024

Call Sign: KB3SPY
Kristen R Schell
1301 M St NW Apt 910
Washington DC 20005

Call Sign: KA3TSV
William T Phillips
3421 M St NW 1245
Washington DC 20007

Call Sign: KB3WRA
Juliet Vogel
1718 M St NW 345
Washington DC 20036

Call Sign: W2JXV
Juliet Vogel
1718 M St NW 345
Washington DC 20036

Call Sign: WI6W
John L Breckenridge
910 M St NW Apt 609

Washington DC 20001

Call Sign: KA3BWY
Sam J Turnbull
430 M St SW 304
Washington DC 20024

Call Sign: WA6UYR
Jeffrey A Sacks
4840 Mac Arthur Blvd NW B104
Washington DC 20007

Call Sign: KB3NCW
Judah H Milgram
4465 Macarthur Blvd NW Apt 101
Washington DC 200072525

Call Sign: KB1QKZ
Michael T Barone
2710 Macomb St NW Apt 205
Washington DC 20008

Call Sign: N3JAY
Richard M Robin
2936 Macomb St NW
Washington DC 20008

Call Sign: KB3DWB
Walter G Birkel
3514 Macomb St NW
Washington DC 20016

Call Sign: KB3QIV
Eric J Kirby
102 Madison St NW
Washington DC 20011

Call Sign: N3RCZ
Troy A John
1229 Madison St NW
Washington DC 20011

Call Sign: KA3OGI
Keith W Calhoun-Senghor
1429 Madison St NW

Washington DC 20011

Call Sign: KB3GBN
Renford G Ellis
922 Madison St NW 302
Washington DC 20011

Call Sign: KA3IYZ
John W Wingo Jr
5322 Manning Pl NW
Washington DC 20016

Call Sign: KA3UNZ
Michael A Cunningham
1616 Marion St NW 105
Washington DC 20016

Call Sign: KB1WS
Timothy B Hanson
814 Maryland Ave NE
Washington DC 200025306

Call Sign: KB3TEX
American University Amateur Radio Club
4400 Mass Ave NW
Washington DC 20016

Call Sign: KB3TFD
American University Amateur Radio Club
4401 Mass Ave NW
Washington DC 20016

Call Sign: WA1U
American University Amateur Radio Club
4402 Mass Ave NW
Washington DC 20016

Call Sign: N3FWR
S Chris Spiliopoulos
4200 Mass Ave NW 701
Washington DC 20016

Call Sign: KB3IKQ
John R Paul
4410 Massachuetts Ave NW 301

Washington DC 20016

Call Sign: K3RJA
Elliot N Sivowitch
2122 Massachusetts Ave NW
Washington DC 20008

Call Sign: AA3SH
Nobutaka Takeda
2520 Massachusetts Ave NW
Washington DC 200082869

Call Sign: AA3ZC
Gerhard Wahlers
2005 Massachusetts Ave NW
Washington DC 20036

Call Sign: KB3VDQ
Michael S Orme
4410 Massachusetts Ave NW 299
Washington DC 20016

Call Sign: N1KYT
Thomas L Devlin
450 Massachusetts Ave NW Apt 303
Washington DC 20001

Call Sign: KB3NAM
Nobuko Takeda
4100 Massachusetts Ave NW A 1103
Washington DC 20016

Call Sign: AB3FC
Nobuko Takeda
4100 Massachusetts Ave NW A 1103
Washington DC 20016

Call Sign: K3FGB
Morton Slavin
4000 Massachusetts Ave NW Apt 1322
Washington DC 20016

Call Sign: WB4YEZ
Allison T French
1349 Massachusetts Ave SE

Washington DC 200031540

Call Sign: KB3IQM
Juan Fanals
1410 Massachusetts Ave SE
Washington DC 20003

Call Sign: N3CQR
Arthur J Hill
1728 Massachusetts Ave SE
Washington DC 20003

Call Sign: KT4DX
James C Gray III
300 Massachusetts Avenue NW
Washington DC 20001

Call Sign: KA3ZJJ
Kelly C Degnan
2920 McKinley NW
Washington DC 20015

Call Sign: KB3JFM
Sherrod A Ross
39 Michigan Ave NE
Washington DC 20002

Call Sign: W3WDC
Vincent M Destajo
3332 Military Rd NW
Washington DC 200151722

Call Sign: WB2ZXZ
Alan B Rosenfeld
4301 Military Rd NW Apt 303
Washington DC 200152088

Call Sign: KB3IYD
Bobby M Mcfadden
2316 Minnesota Ave SE
Washington DC 20020

Call Sign: N2FOA
Jonathan F August
1863 Mintwood Pl NW 3

Washington DC 20009

Call Sign: KB3FFV
Carolyn A Ward
174 Mississippi Ave SE A
Washington DC 20032

Call Sign: KB3BVY
Walter L Marshall
1824 Monroe NW
Washington DC 20010

Call Sign: WB0YRY
Thomas C Murphy
1243 Monroe St NE
Washington DC 20017

Call Sign: KB0URZ
Walter M Plush
1491 Morris Road SE
Washington DC 20020

Call Sign: KF4WKL
Matthew W Ashburn
1412 Morse St NE
Washington DC 20002

Call Sign: KB6ZN
Herbert Jeffries
3700 N Capitol St NW   1076
Washington DC 200118400

Call Sign: N4TCW
Leon S Ciereszko III
126 N Carolina Ave SE
Washington DC 20003

Call Sign: N3OSA
Lucille M Ponze
3700 N Capital St NW
Washington DC 20317

Call Sign: KB3MEO
 Afrh-W Amateur Radio Association
3700 N Capital St NW   1319

Washington DC 200118400

Call Sign: AF3RH
 Afrh-W Amateur Radio Association
3700 N Capital St NW   1319
Washington DC 200118400

Call Sign: K4TBC
Terry W Sawyer
3700 N Capital St NW Apt 110
Washington DC 20317

Call Sign: W4OSF
Earl L Backus
3700 N Capitol St
Washington DC 20317

Call Sign: WD6ENR
Budd W Jackson
3700 N Capitol St NW
Washington DC 20011

Call Sign: KB3BEM
Michael P Gallagher
3700 N Capitol St NW
Washington DC 20317

Call Sign: W3FDM
Eddie L Rainey
3700 N Capitol St NW
Washington DC 203179998

Call Sign: KB3LAA
Raymond R Anderson
3700 N Capitol St NW
Washington DC 20317

Call Sign: KB3KWC
Donald L Russell
3700 N Capitol St NW 126
Washington DC 200118400

Call Sign: KB3KZY
John P Davies Jr
3700 N Capitol St NW 368

Washington DC 20317

Call Sign: NG4Y
Carrol W Collins
3700 N Capitol St NW 775
Washington DC 200118400

Call Sign: KE4TBC
Terry W Sawyer
3700 N Capitol St NW Apt 110
Washington DC 20317

Call Sign: KH6ILR
Allan C Hubbert
3700 N Capitol St NW No 1111
Washington DC 20011

Call Sign: KB3KZZ
Charles L Bronson
2700 N Capitol St NW Usr 595
Washington DC 203170001

Call Sign: N3DRT
Enoch C Stephens
3700 N Capitol St NW Ussah
Washington DC 20317

Call Sign: KB3TNM
Russell L Miller Jr
1605 N Portal Dr NW
Washington DC 200121012

Call Sign: W5FET
David N Shelby
1205 N St NW Unit E
Washington DC 20005

Call Sign: AD6IU
Richard W Obermayer
1000 N St NW Apt B
Washington DC 20001

Call Sign: WA1MAH
John L La Brecque
470 N St SW

Washington DC 20024

Call Sign: W3HDO
George M White
3337 N St NW
Washington DC 20007

Call Sign: KC6SBI
Richard C Johnson
2130 N St NW Apt 109
Washington DC 20037

Call Sign: KA3TOC
Omari A West
134 N St SE
Washington DC 20020

Call Sign: KA3TOD
Tony A Murray
520 N St SW
Washington DC 20024

Call Sign: N3GE
Anthony M Gates
510 N St SW Apt N232
Washington DC 200244526

Call Sign: KB3FTJ
Mary M Rozelle
520 N St SW S26
Washington DC 20024

Call Sign: K3EEG
Elizabeth Bentley
5010 Nash St NE 1
Washington DC 20019

Call Sign: N3CGN
Thomas A Nash
2804 Naylor Rd SE Apt B124
Washington DC 20020

Call Sign: N3WFA
James H Carlton
1168 Neal St NE

Washington DC 20002

Call Sign: N3FRT
Robert D Haslach
5516 Nebraska Ave NW
Washington DC 20015

Call Sign: WB3KGZ
Salvador C Fulgueras
5400 Nevada Ave NW
Washington DC 20015

Call Sign: N3QJU
Richard E Morse
5530 Nevada Ave NW
Washington DC 20015

Call Sign: WB1CPA
Robert A Morse
5530 Nevada Ave NW
Washington DC 20015

Call Sign: KF4UNA
Nico C Kalteis
1735 New Hampshire Ave NW 304
Washington DC 20009

Call Sign: W3NCK
Nico C Lacchini
1735 New Hampshire Ave NW 304
Washington DC 20009

Call Sign: W3NCL
Nico C Lacchini
1735 New Hampshire Ave NW 304
Washington DC 20009

Call Sign: WB6WDS
Douglas A Heydon
1751 New Hampshire Ave NW
Washington DC 20009

Call Sign: KA3WXC
Bruce L Dunn
1924 New Hampshire Ave NW

Washington DC 20009

Washington DC 20007

Call Sign: KB3FHP
Jeffrey Norman
4931 New Hampshire Ave NW
Washington DC 20011

Call Sign: K3DOC
 Department Of Commerce Amateur Radio
Society
1212 New York Ave NW Ste 600
Washington DC 20005

Call Sign: AA3WP
Jeffrey Norman
4931 New Hampshire Ave NW
Washington DC 20011

Call Sign: N1OOX
Nicholas A Goad
1353 Newton St NW
Washington DC 20010

Call Sign: KB3ITM
Porsche N Norman
4931 New Hampshire Ave NW
Washington DC 20011

Call Sign: N3VXX
Radcliffe A Harewood
2235 Newton St NE
Washington DC 200183072

Call Sign: WD4SGZ
Stephan F Woolley Sr
4843 New Hampshire Ave NW 4
Washington DC 20011

Call Sign: KB3TEA
 Hacdc
1525 Newton St NW
Washington DC 20010

Call Sign: WA3VGZ
William F Montgomery
700 New Hampshire NW
Washington DC 20036

Call Sign: W3HAC
 Hacdc
1525 Newton St NW
Washington DC 20010

Call Sign: W3GGF
Warren G Mullen
1618 New Jersey Ave NW
Washington DC 20001

Call Sign: N3MNZ
Donald D Lampkins
621 Nicholson St NW
Washington DC 20011

Call Sign: KB3PDS
Janet Worthington
435 New Jersey Ave SE
Washington DC 20003

Call Sign: N3ZGM
Edwin C Gonzalez Alexander
1361 Nicholson St NW 1
Washington DC 20011

Call Sign: K1CCC
John L Heyl
2801 New Mexico Ave Apt 901
Washington DC 20007

Call Sign: W4NJZ
Mark A Cordover
2610 Normanstone Ln NW
Washington DC 20008

Call Sign: K8HIQ
Raymond L Hayes
2801 New Mexico Ave NW

Call Sign: AA3QO
Yoshie Oshima

330 Ntl Pre Bld 14 & F NW
Washington DC 20045

Call Sign: KB4FBV
Rikkie O Canada
216 O St SW 20
Washington DC 20024

Call Sign: WA4BCW
Ralph A Taylor Jr
57 Observatory Cir NW
Washington DC 20008

Call Sign: W3MI
Philip M Matthews
645 Oglethorpe St NE
Washington DC 20011

Call Sign: KD4WGL
Haisam K Ido
3123 Oliver St NW
Washington DC 200151654

Call Sign: N1CGF
Michael Kiron
3219 Oliver St NW
Washington DC 20015

Call Sign: W3DCA
Michael Kiron
3219 Oliver St NW
Washington DC 20015

Call Sign: N3BNO
Eugene T Hall
2300 Ontario Rd NW
Washington DC 20009

Call Sign: WA3ZKD
Glenn W Forman
2820 Ordway St NW
Washington DC 20008

Call Sign: KO3C
Geoffrey Cheadle

6200 Oregon Avenue NW Apt 106
Washington DC 20015

Call Sign: KB8FOX
Darian K Lewis
3034 Otis St NE
Washington DC 200182934

Call Sign: WA3YEU
Gerald W Kinzelman
1415 Otis St NE
Washington DC 20017

Call Sign: KA3ZOX
Matthew Whitfield
1434 Otis St NE
Washington DC 20017

Call Sign: W3NKF
Nrl Amateur Radio Club
4555 Overlook Ave SW
Washington DC 20375

Call Sign: N3OQJ
George A Hansen
2130 P St NW 824
Washington DC 20037

Call Sign: KB3JBY
Igor A Chell
9100 Panama City Pl
Washington DC 205219100

Call Sign: KB2USK
C Federico Campbell
1020 Papermill Ct NW
Washington DC 20007

Call Sign: KB3JBZ
Robert H Kirk
9200 Paris Pl
Washington DC 201899200

Call Sign: KA3SHK
Gregory M Coombs

3518 Park Pl NW
Washington DC 20010

Call Sign: W3IWN
Benjamin Schiffer
3125 Patterson St NW
Washington DC 20015

Call Sign: KB3MEG
District Of Columbia Amateur Radio
Society
3511 Patterson St NW
Washington DC 20015

Call Sign: NW3DC
District Of Columbia Amateur Radio
Society
3511 Patterson St NW
Washington DC 20015

Call Sign: W3DQ
Eric Rosenberg
3511 Patterson St NW
Washington DC 20015

Call Sign: W1NTX
Harold S Nagle
3605 Patterson St NW
Washington DC 20015

Call Sign: N3IZP
Robert J Moore
330 Peabody St NE
Washington DC 200111644

Call Sign: KB3JXO
Natalie N Barbour
3304 Pennsylvania Ave 206
Washington DC 20020

Call Sign: KI6UKY
Graig L Cropper
2020 Pennsylvania Ave NW
Washington DC 20006

Call Sign: KA3KPF
Dorothy J Black
2555 Pennsylvania Ave NW 602
Washington DC 200371613

Call Sign: KB8RIQ
Mike I Nartker
2400 Pennsylvania Ave NW 701
Washington DC 20037

Call Sign: N3QEM
Stephen E Schmidt
935 Pennsylvania Ave NW Box 33
Washington DC 20535

Call Sign: K3WLA
Ronald M Thomas
3304 Pennsylvania Ave SE   112
Washington DC 20020

Call Sign: W9ALZ
Stephen G Smith
1000 Perry St NE Apt 9
Washington DC 20017

Call Sign: WA3UGU
Richard C Leahy
2006 Plymouth St NW
Washington DC 20012

Call Sign: N3KRL
John W Ruser
3539 Porter St NW
Washington DC 200163177

Call Sign: N3AQG
Ken D Williams
3251 Prospect St NW   406
Washington DC 20007

Call Sign: KB3SYL
Luca Nerva
4445 Q St
Washington DC 20007

Call Sign: W1FZR
Luca Nerva
4445 Q St
Washington DC 20007

Call Sign: KC6RAY
Barney W Gimbel
1615 Q St NW 601
Washington DC 20009

Call Sign: WB2LCT
Robert T Mc Kinley
2527 Q St NW 206
Washington DC 20007

Call Sign: KA3EIH
Charles D Reed
1310 Q St NW
Washington DC 20009

Call Sign: KC2BAN
Tanya E Balsky
2501 Q St NW
Washington DC 20007

Call Sign: N3FXE
John C Johnson
2500 Q St NW 234
Washington DC 20007

Call Sign: KA3NIT
Robert C F Gordon
4436 Que St NW
Washington DC 20007

Call Sign: W3BAS
Donald H Saunders
4922 Quebec St NW
Washington DC 20016

Call Sign: W3POB
Walter W Pepmiller
2800 Quebec St NW Apt 847
Washington DC 20008

Call Sign: W9QU
James F Edmiston
1400 Quincy St NE
Washington DC 20017

Call Sign: W3OFM
James F Edmiston
1400 Quincy St NE
Washington DC 20017

Call Sign: KA3GKT
Levernard A Speight
710 Quincy St NW
Washington DC 20011

Call Sign: N2CXX
William Dixon
3537 R St NW
Washington DC 20007

Call Sign: N1WPD
David M Rosner
1830 R St NW Apt 23
Washington DC 20009

Call Sign: AB3AZ
Philip D Kohn
1830 R St NW Apt 31
Washington DC 20009

Call Sign: KB3LAC
Sarah E Clarke
527 Randolph St NW
Washington DC 20011

Call Sign: W3ACE
Armin H Meyer
4610 Reno Rd NW
Washington DC 20008

Call Sign: AA3RQ
Geoffrey L Barrows
4905 Reno Road NW
Washington DC 20008

Call Sign: N3NQC
Juanita E Carter
1322 Riggs St NW
Washington DC 20009

Call Sign: K3ZDC
William S Murray
1509 S St   NW
Washington DC 20009

Call Sign: KF6SO
Terry D Garcia
3507 Rittenhouse St NW
Washington DC 20015

Call Sign: KB3YAZ
Erskine Phillips
1920 S St SE
Washington DC 20020

Call Sign: KF3ES
Terry D Garcia
3507 Rittenhouse St NW
Washington DC 20015

Call Sign: KB3QDB
Annette K Schoonover
63 S St NW
Washington DC 20001

Call Sign: WA0PMT
Robert E Keith
3207 Rittenhouse St NW
Washington DC 20015

Call Sign: W3VAV
Roger W Montague
3545 S St NW
Washington DC 20007

Call Sign: KB3UJQ
Martin R Rothfield
4215 River Road NW
Washington DC 20016

Call Sign: N3EPH
Cyrus C Parker
1505 Saratoga Ave NE
Washington DC 200182021

Call Sign: N3QDT
James T Lumpkins
125 Rock Creek Church Rd NW
Washington DC 20011

Call Sign: KD3XI
Eugene F Bernard
910 Savannah St
Washington DC 20032

Call Sign: K3UAM
Clement R Williams
3624 Rock Creek Church Rd NW
Washington DC 200101537

Call Sign: WA3KQV
Stephen J Havilland
1 Scott Cir NW
Washington DC 20036

Call Sign: KA3GNN
John P Coyle
3319 Rowland Pl NW
Washington DC 20008

Call Sign: W3PK
Perry I Klein
700 Seventh St SW
Washington DC 20024

Call Sign: NG3D
James A Walker
3506 Runnymede Pl NW
Washington DC 200152420

Call Sign: W3ZM
 Radio Amateur Satellite Corp
700 Seventh St SW 226
Washington DC 200242484

Call Sign: NU5Z
Jeffrey W Koch
515 Seward Square SE 6J
Washington DC 20003

Call Sign: N3MVI
Abeeku M Clark
2251 Sherman Ave NW 1025E
Washington DC 20001

Call Sign: NV1P
Kennan B Low
5424 Sherrier Pl NW
Washington DC 200162562

Call Sign: KE3X
Kennan B Low
5424 Sherrier Pl NW
Washington DC 200162562

Call Sign: KB3VAU
Palisades Radio Club
5424 Sherrier Pl NW
Washington DC 200162562

Call Sign: K3PRC
Palisades Radio Club
5424 Sherrier Pl NW
Washington DC 200162562

Call Sign: NW3O
Palisades Radio Club
5424 Sherrier Pl NW
Washington DC 200162562

Call Sign: K3PRC
Palisades Radio Club
5424 Sherrier Pl NW
Washington DC 200162562

Call Sign: KB3SPI
Aidan M Low
5424 Sherrier Pl NW
Washington DC 20016

Call Sign: KB3RUP
Kody B Low
5424 Sherrier Pl NW
Washington DC 20016

Call Sign: K3ODY
Kody B Low
5424 Sherrier Pl NW
Washington DC 20016

Call Sign: KB3RUO
Patrick A Low
5424 Sherrier Pl NW
Washington DC 20016

Call Sign: K3PAL
Patrick A Low
5424 Sherrier Pl NW
Washington DC 20016

Call Sign: N3LCA
Stuart O Spransy
8 Snows Ct NW
Washington DC 20037

Call Sign: KB3DLY
Dc Contest Team
21 St NW 720 Rite 1133
Washington DC 20036

Call Sign: W1BT
Antique Wireless Club
22 St NW 720 Rite 1133
Washington DC 20036

Call Sign: K3MU
Uotome Motoaki Arc
21 St NW 720 Rite 1133
Washington DC 20036

Call Sign: KB3JTC
Kelvin Lewis
1424 Staples St NE Apt 4
Washington DC 20002

Call Sign: K4OJU
Milton K Mills
3227 Stephenson Pl NW
Washington DC 200152457

Call Sign: AA3MD
Craig J Sterling
3233 Stephenson Pl NW
Washington DC 20015

Call Sign: KB3YER
Leonard M Munyao
1702 Summit Pl NW 209
Washington DC 20009

Call Sign: WB2GIN
Paul Taylor
1713 Surrey Ln NW
Washington DC 20007

Call Sign: N3RDX
Samudra E Haque
1631 Suter Lane NW
Washington DC 20007

Call Sign: N3JMP
Austen B Iduwe
1439 T St NW Apt 203
Washington DC 20009

Call Sign: KB3JRY
Michael E Skehan
1679 Tamarack St NW
Washington DC 20012

Call Sign: N3QPR
James A Washington
0 Taylor St NE Apt 24
Washington DC 20017

Call Sign: KA4MCL
Henry S Newport
1875 Taylor St NW
Washington DC 20011

Call Sign: K6LEW
Owen Wormser
3201 Tennyson St NW
Washington DC 20015

Call Sign: KB3KZA
 Microwave Beacon Builders Club - Dc
3201 Tennyson St NW
Washington DC 20015

Call Sign: W3BIN
Robert L Lannen
2712 Terrace Rd SE Apt 606
Washington DC 20020

Call Sign: KA3HHN
Doxy J Holt
616 Tewkesbury Pl NW
Washington DC 20012

Call Sign: K2EUL
Elliott J Moulton
1061 Thomas Jefferson St NW
Washington DC 20007

Call Sign: NP2FV
Jane S Frantz
613 Tuckerman St NW
Washington DC 20011

Call Sign: N3VUT
Lawrence G Mc Donough
3900 Tunlaw Rd NW 604
Washington DC 20007

Call Sign: KB3OEX
Richard J Sawyer
2610 Tunlaw Rd NW Apt 1
Washington DC 20007

Call Sign: W3HPF
George V Kinal
3303 Upland Terr NW
Washington DC 20015

Call Sign: KA3WTQ
David W Beaubien
3669 Upton St NW
Washington DC 20008

Call Sign: AA3MN
Thomas D Taylor
3720 Upton St NW
Washington DC 20016

Call Sign: KE3BV
Leonard Finkle
0 Ussah
Washington DC 20317

Call Sign: KB3PPX
Cameron P Finucane
5724 Utah Ave NW
Washington DC 20015

Call Sign: KE3VV
David A Splitt
6111 Utah Ave NW
Washington DC 200152461

Call Sign: KB3QZY
Douglas S Kinney
3607 Van Ness St NW
Washington DC 20008

Call Sign: AG4VE
Shawn R Wilson
2939 Van Ness St NW
Washington DC 20008

Call Sign: N1RLE
Laura J Mizner
2939 Van Ness St NW 346
Washington DC 20008

Call Sign: KC2BET
Richard I Cohen
2950 Van Ness St NW Apt 627
Washington DC 20008

Call Sign: WB3LSR
Albert J Barr
3729 Van Ness St NW
Washington DC 20016

Call Sign: N3ZMT
Robert N Lumpkin
3003 Van Ness St NW 5 1022
Washington DC 200084742

Call Sign: W3FOI
Harry H Herman Jr
3003 Van Ness St NW 204 S
Washington DC 20008

Call Sign: N3YIE
Matthew J Powers
3003 Van Ness St NW Apt W409
Washington DC 20008

Call Sign: WA3LKF
Stanley M Clasen
3003 Van Ness St NW S525
Washington DC 200084704

Call Sign: KP4DJX
Beale E Riddle Jr
3003 Van Ness St NW S-712
Washington DC 200084712

Call Sign: N3RDC
John T Korman
3001 Veazey Terr NW
Washington DC 200085412

Call Sign: N3AER
Sally J Smith
3001 Veazey Terr NW 410
Washington DC 20008

Call Sign: W3HST
William H Smith
3001 Veazey Terr NW 410
Washington DC 20008

Call Sign: KF4CHO
Robert J Hohmann
1825 Vermont Ave NW
Washington DC 20001

Call Sign: NF3CC
Inc. National Frequency Coordinators
Council
1090 Vermont Ave NW Ste 910
Washington DC 20005

Call Sign: K5MG
Michael P Glover
2440 Virginia Ave NW Apt D-1201
Washington DC 20037

Call Sign: N3EMP
Eugene L Bialek
2700 Virginia Ave NW Apt 410
Washington DC 20037

Call Sign: KB3JVQ
Clarence E Bostic
400 Virginia Ave SW 110
Washington DC 20024

Call Sign: KB3NZC
Donald H Harter
2475 Virginia Avenue NW 503
Washington DC 20037

Call Sign: N3DPD
George Abraham
3107 W over Dr SE
Washington DC 20020

Call Sign: N3ECI
Samuel F Nelson Sr
1530 W St NE
Washington DC 20018

Call Sign: N3KOY
Dorothya L Grant
3207 W St SE
Washington DC 20020

Call Sign: KC0GDD
Jonathan M Newport
3227 Walbridge Pl NW
Washington DC 20010

Call Sign: N3DZQ
Plater T Campbell
1234 Walter St SE
Washington DC 20003

Call Sign: KB3KFZ
Cynthia Shields
3114 Warder St NW
Washington DC 200102919

Call Sign: KB3KGC
Evonne D Greene
3114 Warder St NW
Washington DC 200102919

Call Sign: N3UNG
Raul A Fuentis
3312 Warder St NW
Washington DC 20010

Call Sign: N3ZGK
Juan M Chavez
3312 Warder St NW
Washington DC 20010

Call Sign: N3ZGL
Jose E Fuentes
3312 Warder St NW
Washington DC 20010

Call Sign: KB3MNV
Michael B Hawes
416 Warner St NW
Washington DC 20001

Call Sign: KB3WAZ
Keith E Daegele
249 Warren St NE
Washington DC 20002

Call Sign: KB3JLF
Derek Riker
260 Warren St NE
Washington DC 20002

Call Sign: KB3WAF
Philip N Johnson
1000 Water St SW 21
Washington DC 20024

Call Sign: KB9JIC
Marcy A Downes
1000 Water St SW 78
Washington DC 20024

Call Sign: KB3WYW
Mark Grabowsky
600 Water St SW Nbu 3-7
Washington DC 20024

Call Sign: KB3WCY
Christopher W Snow
1000 Water St SW 23
Washington DC 20024

Call Sign: KB3LGG
William D Barr
1000 Water St SW 43
Washington DC 20024

Call Sign: KB3WDR
Paul G Evans
1000 Water St SW 57
Washington DC 20024

Call Sign: KA3QEC
Elizabeth R Campfield
600 Water St SW Nbu1-6
Washington DC 20024

Call Sign: KB3WZA
 Capital Yacht Club Amateur Radio Club
1000 Water St SW Ste 37
Washington DC 20024

Call Sign: W3CYC
 Capital Yacht Club Amateur Radio Club
1000 Water St SW Ste 37
Washington DC 20024

Call Sign: W7KJD
Gordon S Creed
6917 Western Ave NW
Washington DC 20015

Call Sign: KB8UUM
Geoffrey B Storchan
905 Westminster St NW Apt 2
Washington DC 20001

Call Sign: AB3UM
Geoffrey B Storchan
905 Westminster St NW Apt 2
Washington DC 20001

Call Sign: KB3PUV
Alfonso Alberino
3000 Whitehaven NW
Washington DC 20008

Call Sign: N3UCF
Gail L Juppenlatz
3542 Whitehaven Pky NW
Washington DC 20007

Call Sign: AA3FH
Richard M Juppenlatz
3542 Whitehaven Pky NW
Washington DC 20007

Call Sign: N3HFH
Kim Jorgensen
3200 Whitehaven St NW
Washington DC 20008

Call Sign: K6IDN
Arnold J Lipman
1728 Wisconsin Ave NW 101
Washington DC 20007

Call Sign: KB3TAG
Juliana Neelbauer
3601 Wisconsin Ave NW 204
Washington DC 20016

Call Sign: WA3JR
Jean L Rehbock
2500 Wisconsin Ave NW 803
Washington DC 200074517

Call Sign: KC0GLX
Ken J Ambrose
2712 Wisconsin Ave NW Apt 910
Washington DC 20007

Call Sign: AA0CR
Richard S Garrett
2500 Wisconsin Ave NW Apt 305
Washington DC 20007

Call Sign: WD3G
William R Meyn
2201 Wisconsin Ave NW Apt 515
Washington DC 20007

Call Sign: WP4NYL
Miguel A Garcia-Garcia
2800 Wisconsin Ave NW Apt 909
Washington DC 20007

Call Sign: KV3H
Miguel A Garcia-Garcia
2800 Wisconsin Ave NW Apt 909
Washington DC 20007

Call Sign: KB2LTR
John A Evanoff
2618 Woodley Pl NW
Washington DC 20008

Call Sign: WA2LQH
Richard A Solomon
3126 Woodley Rd NW
Washington DC 20008

Call Sign: N3HUL
Paul H Berkowitz
3715 Woodley Rd NW
Washington DC 20016

Call Sign: KA3PQD
Steve J Volchko
2660 Woodley Rd NW Apt 5300
Washington DC 20008

Call Sign: KA3PQC
Steven J Volchko
2660 Woodley Rd NW Ste 5300
Washington DC 20008

Call Sign: KB9YTQ
Mark D Winek
2800 Woodley Road NW Apt 234
Washington DC 200084116

Call Sign: WA3MHA
William D Weber
2301 Wyoming Ave NW
Washington DC 20008

Call Sign: KB3WRS
Alexander V Skarulis
4215 Yuma St NW
Washington DC 20016

Call Sign: WB2CET
Robert J Haroutunian
0
Washington DC 20008

Call Sign: KA3VKY
Robert A Herring Jr
0
Washington DC 20016

Call Sign: KC3LB
Essex C Noel III
0
Washington DC 20039

Call Sign: KA3SBR
Ray G Laatz
 Aac 1113
Washington DC 20013

Call Sign: KA3SBS
H A Laatz
 Aac 1113
Washington DC 20013

Call Sign: K3MYI
Bruce W Haupt
 Box 21599 Kalorama Station NW
Washington DC 20009

Call Sign: WB4BEN
Anita J Oberholtzer
 Box 37301 Pac 0888
Washington DC 20013

Call Sign: KZ3Y
Prophet Elijah
 Box 50575
Washington DC 20091

Call Sign: WB8ULK
Charles R Thomas
 Box 75500
Washington DC 20013

Call Sign: N3RF
Johan K V Svanholm
 Box 81
Washington DC 20044

Call Sign: N3JNI
Steven G Prindle
 Drawer 19067
Washington DC 20036

Call Sign: K4IAD
 Dulles E-Star Group
 Dulles Airport Ops Ma210
Washington DC 20041

Call Sign: KB3KQR
Lester M Brayshaw
 Foreign Services Loung Dos
Washington DC 205201252

Call Sign: KA3VUN
David N Harrill
 Pac 0542 Box 37301
Washington DC 20013

Call Sign: N3NNS
Brian E Keeney
 Pac 159
Washington DC 20013

Call Sign: WA3SQU
 George Washington Univ Amat Rad Clb
 Sch Of Eng & Appld Sci G W Univ
Washington DC 20052

Call Sign: WB2SDF
Walter D Patterson
 State Dept Libreville Voa
Washington DC 205212270

Call Sign: KB0KEN
Joseph J Hromatka
 US Department Of State Af/Ex/Rover Rm 3517
Washington DC 20520

Call Sign: N0SAS
Joseph J Hromatka
 US Department Of State Af/Ex/Rover Rm 3519
Washington DC 205203517

Call Sign: KD4RP
John J Clinton
 US Embassy Lagos Dos
Washington DC 205218300

Call Sign: KC2IA
Mark L Wenig

Usis Amembassy Addis Ababa St Dept
Washington DC 205212030

Call Sign: W5UYG
John B Van Dyke
 Ussah Box 1632
Washington DC 20317

Call Sign: WA3AQW
James A Murray
 Verplanck Pl NW
Washington DC 20016

Call Sign: N8LBC
Cheryl A Wise
 Voa Colombo Department Of State
Washington DC 205216100

Call Sign: NB3J
Dennis E Heigh
Washington DC 20003

Call Sign: N3MGA
Paulo A Teixeira
Washington DC 20007

Call Sign: N3ZGV
Benito G Anderson
Washington DC 20010

Call Sign: KA3LJR
Christian Kushay
Washington DC 20015

Call Sign: WA8DID
Deanna S Lutz
Washington DC 20024

Call Sign: KB3HSC
Arthur H Lutz
Washington DC 20024

Call Sign: N6NE
Robert D Weller
Washington DC 20026

Call Sign: N3VUD
Frederick L Cranford
Washington DC 20027

Call Sign: N0GEH
Mark E Wise
Washington DC 20032

Call Sign: KA3CXX
Edward R Tyree
Washington DC 20036

Call Sign: N4FK
Francis K Williams
Washington DC 20036

Call Sign: KB3IXX
 Dulles E-Star Group
Washington DC 20041

Call Sign: KA1RDN
John E Aucott
Washington DC 20091

Call Sign: N3YBL
Kelly D Deyoe
Washington DC 200136371

Call Sign: K6CRS
Carl R Swanson
Washington DC 200264474

Call Sign: K8GP
 Delmarva Vhf And Microwave Society
Washington DC 200412307

Call Sign: KA4PXV
Richard J Iliff
Washington DC 200506984

Call Sign: K9TRE
Tareck R Elass
Washington DC 200906503

Call Sign: KE6CUH
Sean E Odenthal
Washington DC 205220303

Call Sign: K6BZB
Amy J Swanson
Washington DC 200264474

Call Sign: W7ACR
Anthony C Rizos
Washington DC 200131013

Call Sign: KB3JXR
Joseph M Proctor
Washington DC 20013

Call Sign: KB3PBZ
Kevin C Stemp
Washington DC 200368923

Call Sign: KB3JCH
Marvin L Patterson
Washington DC 20039

Call Sign: K3MVM
Marvin L Patterson
Washington DC 20039

Call Sign: W3GKV
Michael Quattrone
Washington DC 200138453

Call Sign: KB3VUD
Nicholas D Farr
Washington DC 20013

Call Sign: N0FAR
Nicholas D Farr
Washington DC 20013

Call Sign: KB3SPV
Paul H Berkowitz
Washington DC 20016

Call Sign: KA3VIS

Paul H Berkowitz
Washington DC 20016

Call Sign: KB3QZR
Robert L Taylor
Washington DC 20040

Call Sign: KB3LUA
Susan L Kushay
Washington DC 20015